D0179725

DARE TO
SUCCEED

Experience the Satisfaction
of Doing Business by
the Book

JOE GREENE

FORMER FORTUNE 500 CHIEF OFFICER

WITH GREG WEBSTER

NEW HOPE®
PUBLISHERS
Gospel-Centered. Missions-Driven.

BIRMINGHAM, ALABAMA

New Hope® Publishers
PO Box 12065
Birmingham, AL 35202-2065
NewHopePublishers.com
New Hope Publishers is a division of WMU®.

New Hope Publishers serves its authors as they express their views, which may not express the views of the publisher.

Many of the names in the book have been changed to protect the privacy of those individuals. The author has recalled events and conversations that occurred over the course of his life, and, although they are relayed as accurately as the author can recall them, are not intended to represent word-for-word transcripts. They are intended to convey the essence of an occurrence.

Library of Congress Cataloging-in-Publication Data
Names: Greene, Joe, 1930- author.
Title: Dare to succeed : experience the satisfaction of doing business by the
     book / ; Joe Greene with Greg Webster.
Description: First [edition]. | Birmingham : New Hope Publishers, 2017.
Identifiers: LCCN 2017019147 | ISBN 9781625915276 (permabind)
Subjects: LCSH: Success--Religious aspects--Christianity. | Success in
     business. | Business--Religious aspects--Christianity.
Classification: LCC BV4598.3 .G74 2017 | DDC 248.4--dc23
LC record available at https://lccn.loc.gov/2017019147

ISBN-13: 978-1-62591-527-6

N184101 · 0717 · 2.5M1

"Joe Greene is a true entrepreneur who is passionate about honoring God in the everyday workplace. His book, Dare to Succeed, is bound to help scores of business owners and managers make a real difference in the lives of their customers and employees."

—BOB AUGSBURG, *president, WAY Media Inc.*

"This book illustrates the countless advantages of incorporating biblical principles into your business. Joe Greene's integrity, real-life experiences, and practical advice will encourage, challenge, and help you honor God and serve your stakeholders."

—NANCY REECE, *senior consultant and executive coach,*
The Human Capital Group Inc.

"Too often I hear well-meaning Christians struggle between doing 'good' or being successful in business. Dare to Succeed *reminds us we don't have to choose. Living well and doing good is an attainable goal, and a business run with honesty and integrity is the quickest path to doing both."*

—DAN MILLER, *author and life coach*

"If you haven't found God's career calling on your life, this is the book for you. If you have found God's career calling for your life, then this book is also for you. Joe has written a book that is practical and applicable for all who are discovering God's calling and for those who want to implement this calling in their business and career."

—GLEN CASADA, *Tennessee State Representative*

"Having attended the CEO (Christian Executive Officer) Fellowship that Joe Greene founded, I consider him a mentor. Joe taught me that as Christian business leaders, we should strive to apply biblical principles at our places of business from Monday through Friday. His book, Dare to Succeed, is a compilation of valuable advice and remarkable insight from one of the most influential Christian business leaders of our time."

—MING WANG, *MD, PhD, director, Wang Vision 3D Cataract*
and LASIK Center, Nashville, TN

"It can be done; Joe Greene did it. He operated his company on biblical principles—and it prospered. Not only that, Joe took those principles and trained hundreds of Christian business leaders to do the same. Those of us who have experienced Joe's powerful instruction firsthand celebrate that this teaching is now available to a wider audience. Joe is a fine man of God; you will be inspired, encouraged and equipped to serve God through your business for His Glory."

—SCOTT HARRIS, *missions minister, Brentwood Baptist, Brentwood, TN*

"In a world full of well-meaning but ultimately hollow human advice, it is important to be reminded of the power of 'God's Way' in bringing joy into our leadership, work, and life. Joe Greene really takes us to the heart of the matter!"

—BOB FISHER, *president, Belmont University*

"Most of us live disconnected lives. Our career is in one place and our faith is in another. Most of us find it difficult, if not impossible, to pull the two together into a coherent way of life. Joe Greene shows us not only how to keep our faith and our careers in their proper relationship, but he helps us understand how our faith can provide energy and focus to our careers. The resulting success is not only good for us as individuals but transformative for our companies as well. Joe has written an honest and challenging book about leadership and faith. It's an inspiring read for all of us who want to be successful and not lose our souls in the process."

—DR. MIKE GLENN, *senior pastor, Brentwood Baptist, Brentwood, TN*

"Joe Greene dared to practice what we preach. In Dare to Succeed, he outlines the biblical principles on which executives can operate their business—if they dare! Most of us know the principles but lose them somewhere between idea and execution. Joe not only lays out the principles for all to see, he provides the real-life examples of how God is faithful when we dare to follow Him. Joe challenges each of us to Dare to Succeed, God's way. If you are a leader, this book will teach and inspire you to lead by faith. Read it, if you dare."

—JIM BRYSON, *president, 20Y20 Research Inc.*

DEDICATION

To my dad, A. Roy Greene,

who inspired my life and the accomplishments in this book.

TABLE OF CONTENTS

ACKNOWLEDGMENTS

I honestly thought this book would never happen. A number of people over the years encouraged me to write it and even tried their best to find ways to get it published. But it never seemed to come together until the Lord in His sovereignty was ready for it to happen. I am deeply grateful to all who expressed their desire to have a book authored by me, who prayed for this day to come, and who have cheered me on during the process of getting this book written and published. While I can't possibly name everyone, I would like to especially acknowledge the roles of several who have closely worked by my side to help me fulfill this dream:

First, my wife, Michelle, who kept pushing me to start and finish this book. You are a beautiful and intelligent woman, and I thank you.

My pastor, Mike Glenn, who told me, "Joe, you must write a book."

My assistant, Cheryl Tallyn, who spent many hands-on hours organizing and coordinating the material for this book.

My assistant, Suzanne Alicardi, who found a method for me to dictate the book and to transcribe all my teachings.

My friend, Bruce Loeffer, who introduced me to my collaborator Greg Webster, and to my literary agent, David R. Shepherd. These two men gave me the boost and guidance I needed to write the manuscript and find the publisher.

My editor, Mark Bethea, and his team at New Hope Publishers, who believed in this project and who have done a wonderful job bringing this book to market. My mother Jessie Nolan Greene, a longtime member of the Woman's Missionary Union®, would be proud to know that New Hope published her son's book.

Finally, my longtime friend and business associate, Vicki Tracy, who never ceased to encourage me toward success in business as well as in the writing of this book.

BUSINESS BY *THE* BOOK

My controller stared in disbelief across the conference room table.

"Did that really just happen?"

I spread both palms in front of me and studied the grains in the mahogany surface between them, just to let the moment sink in, then slid my left hand several inches and began flipping the corner of a legal pad on which I had taken notes during the 90-minute meeting.

Mitch said nothing. I stopped flipping pages, slowly looked up at the younger man seated in the leather chair opposite me, and let the barest of smiles creep onto my face.

My company's 37-year-old financial manager shook his head almost imperceptibly. "We don't need his money."

"I know."

"When you first told me to handle our accounts this way, I never expected anything like this."

"I know."

"But if things keep going like they are, there's no limit to what we could accomplish."

"I know."

Mitch straightened his shoulders and contemplated the door through which the president of our largest pharmaceutical supplier had just left.

Then he looked me in the eye. "Did you think something like this would happen?"

"No. I didn't. I had no idea what would come of my change in policy. I only knew it was the right thing to do."

"So I guess it was just one of your 'steps of faith,' right?"

I chuckled at my accounting man's incredulity.

"That's what it was."

Three months earlier, I had told Mitch Taylor I believed our company needed to overhaul the way we handled payments to our vendors. Most companies assume they have 30 days to return payment on an invoice. It allows them to keep money on hand longer—in the bank—and earn interest. But it's really using money that belongs to somebody else. At least that's what I had decided after a passage in Proverbs convinced me of another way to do business. As CEO, I knew I was responsible for making sure we acted corporately in a righteous manner.

That's when I instructed Mitch and his department to pay every vendor invoice within 24 hours of receiving it—or at least by the next business day if the invoice happened to arrive on a Friday. He pointed out that, since our payables could amount to several hundred thousand dollars at any given time, the move would cost us thousands in interest every year. Yet we had just concluded a meeting unlike any other in my 25-year career that provided evidence the revised payables policy was good business.

The president of a major pharmaceutical supplier for my chain of hospitals had flown from Tennessee to our corporate headquarters in Florida for a meeting he requested without an explanation. For the first 15 minutes, we discussed little of consequence. Then he came to the point.

"Joe." He had looked up from his coffee cup and eyed me intently. "Why do you pay my bills as soon as I send you an invoice?"

My explanation was simple: "Because I understand from Proverbs that if I have the money and I know I owe it, then I am to pay it."

The visiting president had then asked more about my plans to run the hospital management company "on so-called Christian principles" and explained his company's financial growth plans. Part of it, he said, involved partnering with other well-run organizations in compatible industries, and he offered a blank check to either invest in my company or to loan us whatever we might need to fund our own growth. Although Mitch and I both declined, he departed with his offer still on the table.

FROM VALIUM TO VISION

When other business people first hear me mention "doing business based on Christian principles," they invariably shake their heads. Some are polite enough not to tell me what they really think of the idea, but others are quite blunt:

"That could never work!"

"What do you mean, *Christian principles?*" (Said with a sneer.)

"Sounds great—if you want to go broke."

"Right, Joe, but nice guys finish last, remember?"

They don't understand that, in the Bible, God reveals His principles of how we should relate to Him and to each other—and that includes how we conduct ourselves in business. Most people are shocked to learn how much the Bible has to say about doing business—and about succeeding by every measure!

I do understand how foreign the idea of Christian business principles sounds to many people. It took me a while to understand exactly how relevant the teachings of the Bible are to making money and succeeding professionally. I'll share a lot of my story as we explore more about doing business God's way, but for starters, let me tell you how long I was in business before I discovered the amazing, business-building, life-enhancing principles I'll share in this book.

By 1980, I had come a long way on a career path in the health-care industry. At the time, Humana was one of the largest hospital management companies in the world, and I was president of operations. I had been a Christian since I was 12 years old and had tried my best to walk faithfully with the Lord. I had worked at Humana for ten years, yet during my last two years an idea began to trouble me. I felt like God was asking me to leave Humana and operate a company on Christian principles.

The idea of using biblical guidelines for business had never occurred to me—and evidently not to anyone else. Although I interacted with hundreds of other high-ranking business people—some I suspected were Christians—no one ever talked about running a company based on concepts in the Bible. Since the idea wouldn't leave me, I decided I would be the one to bring it up.

Whenever the opportunity arose in conversation with one of my colleagues or peers whom I thought of as Christian, I asked what they thought of the idea of running a company based specifically on principles taught in the Bible. Every single one of them said, in so many words, "It won't work. You can't operate a company on Christian principles and be profitable and successful."

Looking back, I'm not sure what they thought those principles were that would cause so much trouble for a business, but at the time, I believed them. So being the faithful servant I am, I reported back to God and told Him, "It won't work."

Evidently, I hadn't gotten quite as clear an understanding of God as I thought. I didn't realize He wasn't looking for my input. He didn't need to have me research the issue and get back to Him. He wanted only one thing from me: cooperation, or as the Bible might call it, obedience. I continued to sense that God wanted me to open, operate, and build a company on Christian principles. I just needed to get started.

The message was clear. I knew what God wanted me to do, but at the time, that wasn't what I wanted to do. My resistance to the idea caused me to live in near misery every day for two years. Taking Valium had not eased my discomfort, and one night in September 1980, extreme high blood pressure landed me in one of our Louisville, Kentucky, emergency rooms. It's handy to be the operations president of the management company running the hospital at a time like that, but the ER doctor offered a stern warning. It seemed to me that he was speaking for God when he told me, "I don't know what's wrong with you, but I can tell you that if you don't correct it, you'll kill yourself."

After release from the hospital the next day, I stood in my kitchen, closed my eyes, and said out loud, "God, I'm going to do what You're calling me to do. I'm going to have to totally depend on You because I have no knowledge of how to do this."

Yielding to God was the prescription I needed. I explained to the Humana board of directors that I would serve as president of operations through the end of the year, but then I was on a new mission. God's provision for implementing His plan began immediately. To show its appreciation for my years of service, the Humana board gave me a generous parting gift, and I left the company with more than enough start-up capital for my new venture—more than twice what I even thought I needed!

Do You Want to Be More Successful than You Are?

Why do God's business principles work? It's the same reason that gravity works—or gestation, changes of season, or any other part of the Grand Design. Business is part of God's creation, a system by which He provides for His favorite creatures: human beings. As such, it operates based on laws or principles built into life. Just as the results from dropping a rock are predictable—the rock falls to the ground—lining up with God's design for economics and finance can also bring predictable results: professional success and personal fulfillment.

I say that, but as I admitted in my story about paying vendors within 24 hours, I didn't know exactly what would happen when I "did the right thing." By that time, I probably should have anticipated something wonderful, but I guess I'm a slow learner. The results of following the principle of not using other people's money improperly for personal gain created an astounding success story for our company.

People too often assume that God doesn't want us to be successful by "worldly standards." We think He will be happier if we live in poverty, so if we're to make lots of money or enjoy the "finer things," we'll have to do that on our own. But not so!

True success is always a matter of accomplishing God's will for your life, no matter where it leads. Some are led to the missions field, for instance. Others are led to create the wealth that can benefit His kingdom. God enjoys blessing His obedient children with abundance in a variety of ways. And some of the most prominent and respected people in the Bible were fabulously wealthy. Think of Abraham, Jacob, David, and—of course!—Solomon. There's nothing wrong with aspiring to be among them. God is comfortable with your ambitions, especially when you are following His guidance. In fact, I'll explain more about how He probably put them there for a purpose, but like the faithful people in Scripture, let's make sure we get first things first.

BE THOU MY VISION

The LORD gave me this message: "I knew you before I
formed you in your mother's womb. Before you were born
I set you apart and appointed you as my prophet to the
nations."

—Jeremiah 1:4–5 NLT

I once posed a simple question to a gathering of 60 chief executive officers from a wide range of businesses: "Are you happy?" The response I received shocked me. Only half of the men in the room claimed to be truly happy.

Knowing the group was made up of professing Christians, I pushed a little deeper and asked, "Do you understand God's vision for you, and are you carrying it out?" This time, a few more answered, "Yes."

It struck me that something was terribly wrong if a group of Christian executives could not articulate God's vision for their life and work and affirm that they were doing specifically what God had called them to do. Worse, perhaps, even fewer of these well-to-do believers were happy. Then it occurred to me that the two observations were related, and a truth emerged in my mind: no matter your level of success, you will not be happy if you are not following God's specific vision for your life. It seemed evident to me that these corporate leaders were going about their business a very wrong way.

PUTTING VISION TO WORK

Imagine hanging a painting on your living room wall. To drive in the nail, you look around for the right tool. The claw hammer is missing from your toolbox, but you find a sledgehammer in the corner of your garage. A hammer is a hammer, right? So you set to work pounding in the nail, but you end up knocking down your living room wall.

It may sound like a ridiculous illustration. Everyone knows that selecting the right tool for a job matters a great deal. When a tool isn't used for its intended purpose, it either destroys what it was meant to improve or it breaks under the strain of something it was not designed to do. Yet that is exactly how most of the executives in the meeting that day were approaching their life's work—and the results showed in the unhappiness and uncertainty in their responses to the questions I asked.

Each of us is a tool in God's hand to do His work here on earth. The difference between the hammers and us, though, is that we get to decide which kind of hammer we're going to be. Will it be the one God intended for the job He has in mind? Or will we ignore the way He's designed us and end up damaging ourselves and those around us in the process? Most of the executives in the room that day had decided, quite apart from God's specific leading, what kinds of tools they would be. So instead of hanging God's masterpiece of a life that declares His glory, they were broken, worn-down, frustrated company officers, little different from their secular counterparts.

The difference that will transform your life into one of fulfillment and joy in God's purpose is having the right vision for your life. Grasping God's vision transforms you into the right tool for the job!

You've no doubt heard the word *vision* countless times. Perhaps you've even read books or attended seminars about it. So what do I mean by vision in the context of trying to operate your business based on Christian principles? In one sentence: vision is a picture of the future that produces godly passion in you.

Notice several key components of this statement. First, vision is a picture. In your mind's eye, you can see something that is your vision. Next, notice that it is in the future. This thing you see hasn't happened yet, but you clearly intend that it will. Why? Because you want it to happen so badly. It produces godly passion in your very soul. The idea of this picture-turned-reality focuses your energy and excitement—your zeal—and provides an adventurous and fulfilling life in return.

It's a wonderful thing when people grab hold of the right vision for their lives. In addition to increasing happiness, it also provides a lens in which to see life in much deeper, more meaningful ways. In 2003, Steve Reinemund, CEO of PepsiCo at the time, told *Theology Today* magazine that his primary goal is to "glorify God and to serve Him in the way that [he is] called to." Reinemund got it! It made him want to go out and do something!

I counted myself a success as the president of operations for Humana and figured I could leave it at that. But God couldn't. In my case, I had stumbled along the path God had for me. After serving as a surgical tech in the Air Force for four years, I wanted no part of the healthcare business. So, what happened? I got an interview for a job as controller at a hospital in Jackson, Tennessee.

My father-in-law arranged my meeting with John Richards, the hospital administrator, and at the meeting, the administrator and I discovered that neither of us wanted to be there. We'd met only as a favor to our mutual connection, my father-in-law, but after two hours, I had accepted a job at the hospital. I didn't understand how well I was made for the healthcare business, but God did. In spite of my own reluctance, I stepped into God's plan for my life. Sometimes His plan comes without warning, and all you can do is walk through the door that opens.

At that point, I couldn't say I had much vision beyond trying to make an honorable living. Years later, though, after I had sufficiently "ripened," God challenged me to a real vision.

Developing a vision is a process. Tom Monaghan, founder of Domino's Pizza, for example, sold his business for $1 billion as the next step in his vision, at age 61. Having lost his father at a young age, Monaghan's mother struggled to provide for Tom and his brother. Consequently, the two boys spent several years in an orphanage before she was able to support them again. Once an adult, Monaghan gorged himself on materialism. He bought antique cars, a helicopter, even the Detroit Tigers baseball team! Yet somewhere along the way, he realized that having stuff wasn't much of a vision. Now he has established a foundation through which he channels his great wealth to minister the gospel to lost people. He's not only at "the top of his game," he's at the top of his vision!

Another way to understand vision is that it lets you know why you were born and what your life is all about. No one's sole purpose is to build an empire for themselves. The CEO life of extravagance produces nothing more than the sin of pride. Getting rich might be enjoyable for a season, but as Tom Monaghan found, giving it away is fulfilling.

If you miss out on the reward of discovering God's vision for your life, you'll end up with a variety of symptoms (perhaps you're experiencing some of them now):

- Physical illness

- Lack of fulfillment

- A general sense of frustration

- Feelings of mediocrity

- Joylessness

- Financial stress

- Family strife

Even the most on-track vision-followers at least temporarily experience most of these problems. If you are a Christian, though, and you experience an ongoing combination of these symptoms in your role as executive, spouse, or parent, it means that somewhere along the way, you started to believe a lie. You started to believe the deception of the devil that God does not have a specific purpose for your life. No matter how outlandish a vision might seem, He can provide what you need to fulfill your God-given vision.

When my job in Jackson led to an opportunity to work at a hospital in Mobile, Alabama, God gave me a lesson in trusting Him that has, ever since, bolstered my confidence in His faithfulness and vision for my life. When our family moved to Mobile, my third son, Gary, was an exuberant, energetic four-year-old. A year later, though, he had degenerated into a lethargic, sickly five-year-old.

We took him to a half dozen specialists before a urologist finally recognized the symptoms of a failing kidney. Relieved to have identified the problem, we gladly accepted the recommended surgery for Gary's condition. But when I took Gary to see the doctor a couple weeks after the operation, my hopes were soon crushed—my young son had continued to exhibit the same symptoms as before.

"Joe," the urologist said, compassion in his voice, "I hate to tell you, but we're going to have to take out Gary's bad kidney, and not only that, the other kidney has also developed some damage we need to correct."

Although I urgently wanted my boy to get well, I told the doctor, "I'd like to keep Gary out of the hospital for a couple of weeks before we do anything. I want my family and friends to pray for him and give him a chance to get a little strength back."

Our surgeon agreed to the delay, so I invited prayers over Gary from local church members, extended family, and assorted Christian friends around the country. After two weeks, I felt God urging me toward a commitment I didn't want to make. Finally, the night before Gary was scheduled to return to the hospital for surgery, I faced up to what I needed to do.

"Lord," I prayed, "whatever Your will is, I accept it. If you have to take Gary from us, I will even accept that." It was the most difficult prayer I had ever prayed.

The next morning began with preparatory Xrays before surgery. Suddenly the room began bustling with several extra radiologists who had been called in to offer opinions of Gary's Xrays. After 15 minutes of quiet but intense conversation among themselves, and anxiety and fear on my part, the radiologist in charge of Gary's case announced, "There's been some mistake. These Xrays are from a kid who's got two normal kidneys. We need to take a new set."

Now I feared hospital management problems in addition to Gary's condition, so I insisted on going to the Xray lab with the technicians. They settled Gary for another series, and I watched the tech take the images, develop them, and hang them on the view boxes. There would be no mistaking whose Xrays were being analyzed.

After another radiologist group discussion with Gary's doctor, the urologist looked at me, confounded. "Joe," he told me, "Your son has two completely normal kidneys. There is no longer a single thing wrong with him."

Praise God was my only thought. Gary was healed.

If you are suffering, it might be encouraging for you to recall just how big God is. He is the God who made heaven, earth, and countless galaxies, the God who parted the Red Sea, the One who heals the sick and raises people from the dead. God knows the number of hairs on your head. He is not limited by your current situation, lack of vision, or feelings of despair. He is faithful and consistent in how He will enrich your life with the correct vision. But there are a few things you should also remember about how He works.

PREREQUISITES FOR A VISION

None of us know how many days we have left in this life. A friend shared with me about a family who lost their healthy, strong 19-year-old son to a tragic accident on the job. No one expects a vibrant young person to leave this life so abruptly, but any day could be the last on earth for any one of us. That's why now is the time to get your vision straight with God. Please don't live out your days and miss the vision God has for you.

You only get one run-through in life, so don't live and die without fulfilling His best for yours. Before we talk about the specific steps to discovering your vision, though, let's take stock of two important prerequisites that must be part of your life.

Prerequisite #1 Be Sure You Are a Christian as Defined by the Bible

Scripture explains the need to believe in Christ's sacrifice in order to be saved. To summarize what is required, read John 1:12–13: "But to all who believed him and accepted him, he gave the right to become children of God. They are reborn—not with a physical birth resulting from human passion or plan, but a birth that comes from God" (NLT).

I've never met a non-Christian who knew God's plans for his or her life. The reason is simple: It's hard to communicate with someone you have never met. Believing a God exists "out there somewhere" is not enough. You have to know His will. Romans 12:2 explains: "Do not conform to the pattern of this world, but be transformed by the renewing of your mind. *Then* you will be able to test and approve what God's will is—his good, pleasing and perfect will" (author's emphasis).

The renewing of our minds means that we want to live in accord with God's purpose and plans. He is the One who does the renewing, and we must allow Him to make the necessary changes in us.

If you need to understand God's will for your life, stop now and commit yourself to Him. Accept that Jesus Christ died for your sins, so you can live forever as part of God's family. Once that's done, the Holy Spirit renews your mind and sets you up for fulfilling God's vision.

Prerequisite #2 Throw Off Any Sin that Is Hindering Your Relationship with God

Even if you have already accepted Christ as your Savior, you may not have made much progress in overcoming sin in your life. God calls believers to live for Him in purity and reverence. If there are sins that still hold you, you cannot fulfill the purpose God wants for you. Your first order of business must be to let God cleanse you of any sins from which you have not repented. After all, if you haven't followed through with what God has already asked of you, how can you expect Him to trust you with more? Here's the solution offered by Hebrews 12:1–2 (author's emphasis):

Let us throw off *everything that hinders* and the sin that so easily entangles. And let us run with perseverance the race marked out for us, fixing our eyes on Jesus, the pioneer and perfecter of faith.

Don't let any sin keep you from the joy of knowing and pursuing a glorious vision for your life.

Once you've met the prerequisites, you're ready to make some real progress toward taking hold of God's vision for you.

PARTNERS, IN TIME

Although I knew in my soul what God had called me to do, telling Humana I would be stepping down from my role as operations president to start a new company was really tough. To be honest, I was scared half to death. I felt like an astronaut cutting his lifeline to the mother ship. As I left the boardroom, I could hardly believe what I had done—but God was just getting started with me.

The day I resigned, I walked down the hall of the executive suite toward my office as steadily as I could. I had drifted by two offices when a voice called to me from the third door on the right. It was Tom, Humana's senior vice president of pharmacy. I stopped and peered into his office.

"Did you call me?"

Tom stood up behind his cherry wood desk and motioned me in. "Joe," he paused, studying my face. "Are you all right?"

I mustered a smile. "Sure, Tom. I'm fine." (I wasn't so sure, but neither was I ready yet to tell him what I'd just done.) "What's on your mind?"

"This may seem a bit out of the blue, but, Joe, if you ever decide to go into business for yourself, I want to be your partner."

I stared in silence at Tom for several seconds. Had he somehow heard my conversation in the chairman's office? We had never discussed anything like this before. "That's a pretty serious suggestion, Tom. I appreciate the vote of confidence, but I don't know that you're financially strong enough to do something like that."

"Actually, Joe, that's exactly what made me think to bring this up with you at the moment." He pointed to his desk. "Come over here, and I'll show you what I mean. I just got my financial statements from the bank."

I crossed the room and stood at the desk of my vice president. He placed the tips of the fingers on his right hand on a set of papers and slid them in front of me. I picked up the handful of sheets and flipped through them. I recognized quickly that, not only was Tom's financial position strong enough to warrant considering him as a partner in my new venture, he was actually stronger at the moment than I was for doing something so "foolish" as starting a new company.

Tom became my first partner and an incredible encouragement to me at the moment I most needed reassurance from God that following His vision was the right thing to do. Although we did not remain together for long—I ended up buying out his half of our company—his confidence in working with me got me started in a big way.

STEPPING INTO YOUR VISION

God is the only One who can reveal to you His will for your life. What you can do, though, is put yourself in position to receive what God has for you. I've identified seven steps you can take to be sure you're ready to hear from God about your vision.

Step #1   Acknowledge that God does have a plan for your life.

God spoke definitively about this to His Old Testament prophet Jeremiah:

The word of the LORD came to [Jeremiah], saying, "Before I formed you in the womb I knew you, before you were born I set you apart; I appointed you as a prophet to the nations."

—Jeremiah 1:4–5

This speaks to the plans the Lord had for Jeremiah specifically, but the principle He introduces in this statement applies to all of us.

Sometimes we get so wrapped up in life that we don't make time to listen to God. We forget that His plans for us are always good, even when we face trials in the process. Instead, we get caught up in a system. We finish school, get a job, start a family, and work hard to provide well. We corrupt our priorities and end up losing our families because we have no sense of purpose. Even if you've considered that God may have a plan in mind for you, you may assume that if you let Him have His way, you'd have to sacrifice an enjoyable life to "go there" with God. Not so!

Do you think God's plan for you is large or small? Since you're reading this book, my guess is that you haven't yet discovered just how big God's plans can be.

If you want to pursue God's vision for your life, you have to stop your misguided, small way of thinking and acknowledge that God does, in fact, have a plan for you (and that it is probably a big one). You also have to admit that you'd like to do more with your life than just make a living and have a mediocre existence. Recognize instead God's ability and desire to carry out a grander purpose through you.

Step #2   Transfer Control of Your Will Over to God.

It's possible to seek God's will but then try to answer your own prayers by setting out on your own to figure things out. Or you might seek God's vision but decide it isn't what you want. Then, however sincere you are, you ignore what He has in mind.

This sort of self-directed pursuit has serious consequences. Your search for God's vision will not work if you don't relinquish the answers to Him. Don't ask God for His vision if you aren't willing to follow through. If you honestly want to pursue God's vision for your life, you have to make up your mind ahead of time that whatever it is, you'll do it. Even if the idea seems far-fetched, move ahead. You'll be delighted to find out what happens next.

Step #3   Recognize God works within you to give you the desire and power to accomplish His plans.

God is a great manager. He made you and knows what motivates you, so you'll want to do the very thing He intends for you to do. I'm not talking about wanting things that are clearly sinful or in some other way obviously outside of what God would want. I mean the good and godly things He has put in your heart. They are things related to your gifts, talents, and aspirations (more about these in the next chapter). You just need to align yourself with God's will, so He can turn you loose. As the psalmist says, "Delight yourself in the LORD; and He will give you the desires of your heart" (Psalm 37:4 NASB).

Step #4   Gather information, seek wise counsel, consider alternatives, and pray.

When you have to make a difficult decision in your business, how do you decide what to do? Do you have a process for systematically sorting through the options? Chances are, you do. Typical, appropriate decision-making involves these factors:

Gather as much information as you can about the decision to be made.

Seek advice from someone who knows you, your company, and the situation well.

Consider the options available to you.

Pray over the decision.

Your pursuit of God's vision should include these elements. Remember, this is not some ethereal, heavenly-minded-but-no-earthly-good concept. God is always working out His purposes, so aligning yourself with His plans is a business decision—the most important one you'll ever make.

Step #5   Begin acting on those desires, and watch for the resources to achieve those plans.

Once you're this far into the process, it's time to test the waters to see if you should proceed. For most visions of this type, you'll need money. It's the primary resource required, but the lack of it shouldn't deter you from taking the next step—at least not at first. Sometimes God wants you to take the first step before He gives you what you need to keep going. In Matthew 6:33, Jesus explains how this works: "But seek first [God's] kingdom and his righteousness, and all these things will be given to you as well."

In this part of Matthew's Gospel, Jesus assures His followers that God will provide for them what they need;

their role is to make God and His Kingdom top priority and not seek after "things." For me, I had to be obedient to God and tell Humana about my plans. Then God provided what I needed, even though I had no idea how my step of faith would work out. I ended up receiving a severance package that provided far more than I could have hoped, and I took on a financially capable business partner!

Step #6   If the resources are not available (or don't become available), assume the desire was not from God or else that now is not the right time.

This follows naturally from Step 5 but bears pointing out. If your "market test" doesn't produce the resources you (and God) know you need, then you'd better hold tight. Don't proceed—at least not right now. You may be on the right track, but God is still getting all the pieces in order so your plans with Him will succeed. If you jump the gun, the results might not turn out well. A lack of resources means either stop altogether or wait.

Step #7   If the resources are there to achieve the desire, then check to see if God gives you peace to continue pursuing the plans.

"You will keep in *perfect peace* those whose minds are steadfast, because they trust in you" (Isaiah 26:3, author's emphasis). If God provides the resources and peace that this is His plan, don't waver. Move on! You have the green light, so get going and don't look back.

THE VISION CHECKLIST

If you think you've done everything to get the right mindset about pursuing God's vision but are still having a hard time grasping the plan, you may need to confirm that you've been thorough in your process. Here's a list of questions God may want you to consider:

1. Are you sure you know God? He knows you, but it needs to go both ways.

2. Do you believe Jesus Christ, the Son of God, has been given all power from God to bless you? This includes having eternal life because of your relationship with Him.

3. Do you really believe God is all-powerful in all areas—including business? Will you trust Him?

4. Will you obey Him?

In summary, God's desire is that you operate your business so people (employees, vendors, customers) come to know Him. God will show you daily through His Word and through prayer how to make this happen. (I also encourage you to meet with other Christian CEOs to assist each other in following these plans.) If you operate your company as your mission, understanding His vision for you, He will instruct you in ways the world will not understand, and you will be successful in the mission He has given you. The Lord will go ahead of you and provide your financial source as well as your key people.

Sound good? I hope so. Let's start getting you lined up with God.

> Review These Relevant Scriptures:
>
> 1 Timothy 2:3–4
>
> Hebrews 2:1–4
>
> Proverbs 16:9; 29:18

2

USING YOUR GIFTS FOR GOD

Do not neglect the spiritual gift you received through the prophecy spoken over you when the elders of the church laid their hands on you.

—1 Timothy 4:14 NLT

Three of my sons and I once made up most of the infield on our church softball team. We played second base, shortstop, third base, and catcher, and all of us were respectable players. But Andy, my second son, was "the great one." Early on, I recognized his special abilities and made sure he had the best baseball bat and glove I could buy him. He went on to excel in high school baseball, and after that, most every team in the local leagues wanted him to play for them. He made the most of the tools I had given him to maximize his natural abilities.

GIFTED FOR A REASON

Our gifts and talents are the things we are naturally good at. Both reflect a natural endowment, innate ability, or an aptitude for doing certain tasks well. Although the terms are nearly interchangeable, "gift" implies that someone has provided the thing to you, and it emphasizes the idea that you didn't come by the thing because of your own work. "Talent" highlights the superiority of your ability to do a particular thing as distinct from another person's capability.

In some endeavors—sports and the arts in particular—natural talent is especially obvious. That was the case with Andy. I knew he was a gifted baseball player. You've also, no doubt, been moved to applaud after a stunning concert, responding to the obvious well-honed talents of the musicians. Perhaps you've stared at a painting in an art gallery and marveled at the skill that created it. But are athletes, musicians, and artists the only people God has gifted with innate abilities that bring glory and honor to Him? Does it take a magnificent symphony to reflect God's glory? A pro batting average consistently over 300? A *Mona Lisa*? Or could it be something as mundane as a perfectly balanced accounting spreadsheet? What about a business whose employees are happy and working as a team because the owner manages them well? Or an operations manager who knows the inner workings of the company like the back of their hand and whose employees have complete confidence in his or her leadership? Are these business folks just ordinary, hardworking people, or are they marketplace artisans using their God-given talents on a different kind of stage? I believe all are equally valuable talents when placed in God's immensely capable hands.

Skills, personality traits, aptitudes, and proclivities are the fibers God used when He knit us together in the womb (Psalm 139:13). Oftentimes, the talents we've been given are key to understanding the vision God has for us. And when we're not working in the areas of our giftedness, it can be a main reason for the unhappiness of missing the vision God has for you. The happiness so many find elusive lies in knowing the One who made you, using the unique gifts and talents He gave you, and fulfilling the purpose He had in mind when He gave you the gifts in the first place.

Someone gives a gift in hopes that it will be used in a meaningful way to bring joy to the user and bless those who see and benefit from its proper use, even if the result is not an avocation or world-changing mission. Some gifts are meant be encouraging and uplifting . . . and not necessary a lifelong pursuit. For instance, I gave Andy his bat and glove with the assumption that he would hit home runs and make double plays, not store it in the closet to gather dust, but neither did I think he'd necessarily become the next Cal Ripken.

After Gary's healing from kidney problems, he too demonstrated prowess in a sport of his own. By age ten, he attracted an audience each time I took him to play golf with me. Many much older, long-time golfers would stop their play just to watch Gary's phenomenal style. Even the golf pro at our course agreed Gary's natural abilities were so superior that he had little to teach my son. Although other interests and commitments wooed him from pursuing a career in golf, he still entertains people who appreciate a finely played round.

The fact is, gifts don't happen by accident. God always has a purpose for the talent you've been given.

GIFTS MEANT TO KEEP ON GIVING

Since God gives talents to people for a reason, the question arises: Are you using your gifts and talents in the way God intended? Is the use of them bringing you joy? Are others being blessed by the way you use your gifts and talents?

Answering these questions probably brings mixed feelings. Certainly the ideal answers are "Yes, yes, and yes," but you may not feel very "ideal" about your real, honest-to-goodness answers. If so, you're not alone. The Gallup research organization's Strengths-Finder 2.0 says:

> Do you have the opportunity to do what you do best every day? Chances are, you don't. All too often, our natural talents go untapped. From the cradle to the cubicle, we devote more time to fixing our shortcomings than to developing our strengths.

Living this way is not good for us—or other people.

In Luke 19:12–27, Jesus tells a parable about the serious problem that results when people don't properly use what they've been given. The story explains that a wealthy king offered three workers an opportunity. Each was given a different amount of money to invest on his behalf. The two who were given larger amounts invested well and received a reward. The one who received the least, though, simply kept the money safe and returned it to the king. The conclusion of the story is stunning:

> [T]he king ordered, "Take the money from this servant, and give it to the one who has ten pounds." "But, master," they said, "he already has ten pounds!" "Yes," the king replied, "and to those who use well what they are given, even more will be given. But from those who do nothing, even what little they have will be taken away."
> —Luke 19:24–26 NLT

In light of Jesus' teaching, I find it rather unnerving to consider the consequences of not using well the gifts I've been given. Finding and appropriately using your gifts and talents is one of the most important things you can do in life. So how do you discover your gifts and talents, and how do you figure out how to put them to the best possible use?

GIFTS AND WHAT TO DO WITH THEM

God isn't into guessing games. He wants you to discover your gifts—probably even more than you want to discover them. So, the first step in discerning your gifts is simply to ask the Giver. Pray, and ask God to reveal what you are best at. You likely already have a lot of clues, but He'll be glad to clarify. And while you're asking, ask other people who know you what they think you do well. Check with co-workers, close friends, parents, siblings, and, of course, your spouse if you're married. Other people will have a perspective on your abilities that you will likely find encouraging.

A little reflection on your past can help identify talents as well. What have you succeeded at before? You've probably worked hard at whatever brought success your way, but chances are, you also excel in areas in which you're working at things you're naturally good at.

I have also found that specially designed personality tests can reveal a great deal about a person's giftedness. These tests provide a refreshingly objective approach to gift discovery. They have no hidden agenda or vested interest in the outcome of your evaluation. They simply reflect your unfiltered aptitudes, strengths, and weaknesses. Many reputable tests are remarkably accessible and can be found online. They're not necessarily free, but the investment you make will be money well spent. Here are a few I recommend:

- Myers-Briggs Type Indicator (myersbriggs.org)

- The Predictive Index (predictiveindex.com)

- Personality I.D. (pidteam.crown.org)

- StrengthsFinder (gallupstrengthscenter.com)

Once you've identified your gifts and talents, you'll want to put them to use in the way God intended. This is part of grabbing hold of God's vision for you, and a thorough analysis of gifts and talents goes a long way toward identifying how God wants to use you. Remember, though, God may still choose to use you in ways that don't seem in line with your gifts, specifically to show that He is the One at work in you.

I've distilled the many possible factors regarding giftedness into eight practices that encompass pretty much everything you need to think about in determining how God wants to use you. You might want to pull out a sheet of paper and write out what each of these considerations brings to mind.

1. Pray, and ask God to reveal His vision for the use of your unique gifts and talents.

2. Consider the most motivating and lively interests you have.

3. Weigh heavily any special concern or passion on behalf of others that God has given you.

4. Bear in mind the direction your academic and technical training has pointed you.

5. Evaluate the doors of service opportunity open to you.

6. Think about the encouragement, counsel, and reinforcement you have received from others.

7. Reflect on the roles and jobs that have given you the greatest sense of satisfaction and gratification.

8. Acknowledge that the Spirit of God may lead you into a venture for which you are not "best qualified." God may want to challenge you to do something that means you will not be operating in your own strength, so you have to rely on His strength to get the job done.

Just like a father isn't going to hand his son a bat and glove and never show him how to use it properly, so too your heavenly Father will not give you talents without showing how to put them to use in a way that brings glory to Him, peace and joy to you, and a blessing to others. I've also found that He will work through your circumstances to make known what you can and can't do, and the lessons sometimes come in surprising ways.

LEARNING THE WAYS OF PROFITABILITY

"I got it!"

I stared at John from the door of his office. "What do you mean, 'I got it'?" In the two years since John hired me during the interview neither one of us wanted, I'd learned he had a penchant for being mysterious at times.

John stood up behind his desk. "I found a hospital that needs us to straighten it out, turn it around, and build a new one."

"Whew. That sounds big. Where is it?"

"Mobile, Alabama. I've already committed to the current administrator that we'll take on the project, and I plan to head down there tomorrow to look into it further. I'll call you with what I find out."

Our impromptu Wednesday morning meeting left me wondering what would come of John's seemingly abrupt decision, but by Tuesday of the following week, I saw firsthand the challenge facing us. As I stood on a downtown Mobile, Alabama, sidewalk, I counted 14 columns across the front of an ancient building looming above me. They appeared to be the only structurally sound part of the two-story edifice. Wooden walkways between the columns sagged visibly. That it was built 30 years prior to the Civil War lent an air of historic charm to the structure, but my thoughts shifted in the direction of the future.

We're supposed to manage this place? I wondered how we would keep the building from collapsing, let alone turn it into a profitable hospital. After a short walk-through, I returned to the motel where John and I were staying.

"Man, John, I wanted a challenge, but this is ridiculous!"

He returned the scowl on my face with a broad grin. "Joe, I didn't invite you down here for an interview and discussion about what we should do. Go back to Tennessee, pull your stuff together, and get on down here. I need you to help me turn this thing around."

I did as John said, but I couldn't imagine a happy outcome to what confronted us in Alabama. Here I was with just two years' experience in my grudgingly accepted healthcare career, and now I was tasked with turning a decaying, 130-year-old hospital into a profitable enterprise. Yet this turned out to be the very stage on which God planned to reveal the gifts He had given me that would set the tone for my business performance in years to come. My first responsibility taught me a critical principle: the ability to collect money is fundamental to the survival—to say nothing of the profitability—of a business.

When John and I took over, the Mobile charity hospital was losing money in just about every way imaginable. But the worst problem was its failure to collect what people owed. It fell to me to correct the situation.

I knew most of the patients lived low on the socioeconomic scale, so I also knew being hard-nosed would not help the situation. Figuring, though, that getting some money was better than getting none at all, I devised an unorthodox plan. If it worked, it would be a win-win situation for both the debtors and the hospital.

I rolled out the strategy by sending a notice to each person who owed money to the hospital. The letter made this offer: No matter what amount of money you owe us, every time you send us a payment, I'm going to credit your account for twice what you pay. For instance, if you pay $100, I'm going to give you credit on your account for $200.

Within the first few weeks, thousands of dollars poured in. John and I were stunned at the amount of money we began to recover for the hospital.

Along with learning how to be appropriately charitable, though, I also learned how not to be taken advantage of. Some people, I discovered, had money but just didn't want to pay up. One such debtor came to my office in person to see what I would do for him. His opening statement raised my suspicions.

"You've got a $5,000 hospital bill filed against me for collection, but that is from my previous marriage. I have a new bride, and we are getting ready to build a new house, so I need that $5,000 debit removed from my account."

I still remember the sincere look the guy gave me, but I was not about to provide hospital funds so he could build a dream house for a new wife.

"Sure," I told him. "I can take the debt off the account for you."

"Oh, I really do appreciate that."

I smiled back at his manufactured sincerity and continued, "All you have to do is pay $5,000, and I'll take it off your account."

That wiped the smile off the man's face, but I had sized him up exactly right. He must have really wanted a new house—and had the money to pay for it—because before he left my office, he wrote a check for $5,000 to pay his bill!

TURNING YOUR TALENTS INTO SKILLS

Our gifts develop as we use them. Both education and on-the-job training can improve the skills that leverage your natural abilities. In fact, practicing and persevering with your talents is one key to success in the vision God has for you.

Of the many guides to honing your God-given talents, none has proven more valuable to the folks I've mentored and me than Myron Rush's book *Managing to Be the Best*. He provides eight straightforward, doable guidelines for growing your gifts, and I've adapted them below. (And I highly recommend that you get a copy of the book and read it thoroughly.)

#1 *Be a learner.*

> A spirit of humility allows you to receive valuable input and learn new ways to accomplish work set before you. Early on at the Mobile charity hospital, I recognized that I didn't know everything I needed to know in order to run the hospital well, so I tried out a few ideas that seemed to make sense and paid attention to what worked and what didn't.

#2 *Seek more responsibility.*

> Increasing responsibility on the job is a great motivator to improve the way you do what you do. At the failing charity hospital, I was in a sink-or-swim situation and was responsible for finding a way to get things "swimming." It became one of many times in my career I had to own responsibility for the situation I was in. The ability to do that is a characteristic executives and business leaders must develop.

#3 *Avoid the "settle for" mentality.*

> If you settle for what was a good use of your talents yesterday, you are missing out on the best God has for you today. Admittedly, I was winging it much of the time at the charity hospital, but I ended up being pretty good at improvising. However, winging it wasn't good enough for my subsequent opportunities. I had to apply what I learned in Mobile so I would not have to wing it in the even weightier situations I faced later.

#4 *Focus on the big picture.*

> Don't get bogged down in minutiae. Stay focused on your larger vision. We had to turn the charity hospital into a profitable operation or it would simply go out of business. The big idea of saving the healthcare center from imploding made even the potentially discouraging job of collecting money a task worth coming to work for each day.

#5 *Be a trainer, not just a manager.*

> Teaching someone else to do what you do best will strengthen your own abilities. I discovered early on that I didn't mind solving problems—an important skill for business leaders—and I found later that teaching others included both instruction and modeling of good problem-solving skills.

#6 Develop and maintain balance in your life.

Excelling in a particular area only has benefit when the rest of your life is in balance. If you lose your family or your witness for Christ because you're too busy maximizing your strengths, you've failed in life's most important roles. You might say I learned this the hard way. The charity hospital presented a challenge I loved, but it consumed me. Balance took me a while to learn.

#7 Always make it on your own merits.

Relying on your own—or someone else's—past successes will never strengthen you. Often, what worked in one instance can fall flat in another. You must stay creative with your solutions. My collections experience made this truth clear. While I was gathering money from people who owed the hospital, our vendors were trying to collect money from the hospital. I thought I had a winning approach when I cautioned the vendors that if they hounded me, I would pay them off and never do business with them again. It worked great. They all backed off—except the farmer who provided eggs for the hospital. I warned him that if I paid him what he was there to collect, I would never buy an egg from him again. A look of relief spread across his face, and he said simply, "I sure would appreciate that." He called me on it, and finding the money to pay him was tough! So, don't get smug about what's gone well for you.

#8 Commit to applying biblical principles of personal ethics.

Building your strengths in a way that doesn't follow biblical teaching does more harm than good. When you're excellent at something, you can be tempted to overpower other people or lord it over them. No one respects a leader who does that to employees, customers, or vendors. Remember Christ's words to the disciples about this: "You know that the rulers in this world lord it over their people, and officials flaunt their authority over those under them. But among you it will be different" (Mark 10:42–43 NLT).

LEVELS OF ADVANCEMENT

Above all, it's important to make sure you see how your gifts and talents fit into the building of God's kingdom. The more committed you are to God's work in the world, the more fulfilling it will be when you put your gifts and talents to work. Your mindset about the priority of the things of God is critical.

As I've examined myself and observed others, I've come to believe there are four levels of commitment you can make to working for God in business. From lowest to highest, they are:

- Level 1—To be a Christian working in the marketplace. Accepting Christ is the essential first step in making a difference in your sphere of influence.

- Level 2—To be a Christian who applies biblical principles in his or her work. As a Christian, you should be "salt and light" in the world (Matthew 5:13–16). Your actions in business should be consistent with what you say you believe (see James 2:14–25).

- Level 3—To be a Christian who does business in the fullness and power of the Holy Spirit. Pray and expect God to guide how you make decisions, treat people, and navigate whatever circumstances you find yourself in business. Then be diligent to follow His leading.

- Level 4—To be a Christian committed to the total transformation of the marketplace. As a Christian, your sphere of influence is the market area in which you do business. You should aspire that your presence on behalf of Christ will make a difference there.

This is a case in which more is better. The more you are committed to God's purposes (the higher you are on the four levels), the greater will be the results—in success, satisfaction, and blessing others—from putting your talents to work.

So, take a moment and consider: What level are you on? If you're not yet at Level 4, are you ready and willing to move up a notch or two? If so, you're in position to do God's will in your work.

Review These Relevant Scriptures:

Hebrews 13:20–21

1 Peter 4:10

2 Peter 1:3

Psalm 139:13–14

Discerning God's Will for Your Business

> Look here, you who say, "Today or tomorrow we are going to a certain town and will stay there a year. We will do business there and make a profit." How do you know what your life will be like tomorrow? Your life is like the morning fog—it's here a little while, then it's gone. What you ought to say is, "If the Lord wants us to, we will live and do this or that."
>
> —James 4:13–15 NLT

The day I resigned from Humana, God affirmed my willingness to follow His leading by providing a business partner within an hour after handing in my resignation. Yet as thrilling as that obvious confirmation was, I knew I needed more help than only one other man could provide. In fact, I had two other key people in mind, so I asked God for help in recruiting them.

A pair of Humana executives had exactly the experience—and personal faith—I thought would be ideal for my start-up. One was so ideal, in fact, that he had just been hired by a competitor. When I called him to propose he come with me instead, he told me there was a moving truck at his house loading up for his relocation. I decided, though, that the final decision wasn't up to either one of us, so I asked him, "What do you think God wants you to do?"

If we were to operate on Christian principles, it certainly meant we would operate based on how we thought God was leading us. Not wanting to belabor the conversation, though, I closed with a simple direction: "You pray about it tonight, and whatever you decide will be fine with me."

He called me back the next morning and greeted me with a question: "Where are we going to set up our new office?"

My other prospect had similarly taken a new job, but he joined us too. It was a three-way confirmation that we were on track with God's will for the venture.

DECIDING TO GET IN LINE WITH GOD

For executives and other business leaders, the big, number-one reason we must know God's will is that we constantly face decisions. Some are mundane but others can make or break the business. Decisions often have far-reaching consequences for our lives and the lives of those we lead. Making good decisions also helps keep you on track with your calling. One by one, decisions bring God's vision for your life into being.

To complicate the seriousness of good decision-making, many times the climate in which decisions must be made is far from ideal. No decision is made in a vacuum, and situations can be complex. You'll probably be familiar with some of the factors that take a toll on effective decision-making:

- A pressing need for action—urgency even when making potentially momentous choices

- The heavy weight of potential consequences

- Inevitable risk

- The deliciously enticing "up-side" of success

- Identifying more than one workable solution

- Quickening degeneration
- A lack of important information

These conditions can paralyze even the best leader, causing indecision, a poor decision made in haste, or moving ahead with an unwise course of action determined more by the emotion of the moment than by sound judgment. If a leader can't manage the pressures appropriately, he or she will miss the chance to make God-honoring decisions and too often be swayed by concerns focused only on personal prestige or material wealth. Yet if we want to build a company and a life true to biblical values, we must set aside our own wills and seek God—and ultimately bring our wills in line with His.

TWO LEVELS OF GOD'S WILL

When people ask the question, "What is God's will for my life?" they often have only one thing in mind. They crave knowing what God wants them to do in a particular situation or choice of direction—"What kind of career should I pursue?" "Whom should I marry?" These are appropriate questions, to be sure, but they don't reflect the entire picture of God's will.

Too often, people overlook the fundamental starting point for discerning God's will for their lives. The biblical reality is that God's will operates on at least two distinct levels. One is what we call His general will, and the other is His specific will. When most people ask the what-is-God's-will question, they're jumping to the specific will without regard to His general will. But if you're going to be an effective Christian business leader, you can't ignore God's general will in your life.

God's general will consists of the unchanging, guiding principles revealed in Scripture that all believers are called to adhere to. His general will is always completely clear because it is revealed in the Bible with the clarity of a news headline. The most obvious example is the Ten Commandments. If you're committing adultery or stealing from the company, for example, you're outside of God's will. Period.

The New Testament adds further detail to our understanding of the general will of God. Ephesians 5:15–20 offers benchmarks to accomplishing a life within God's will:

> Be very careful, then, how you live—not as unwise but as wise, making the most of every opportunity, because the days are evil. Therefore do not be foolish, but understand what the Lord's will is. Do not get drunk on wine, which leads to debauchery. Instead, be filled with the Spirit, speaking to one another with psalms, hymns, and songs from the Spirit. Sing and make music from your heart to the Lord, always giving thanks to God the Father for everything, in the name of our Lord Jesus Christ.

The reason you must get in line with God's general will is it provides direction about His specific will in your day-to-day life. This passage clarifies four aspects of God's general will that apply to business situations.

Avoid Drunkenness

Rely on God to help you face reality rather than escaping into potentially addictive or otherwise harmful behaviors. Scripture never promises that God's will for you and me is to be happy or pain-free. It does say, though, that God wills that we face reality. When we confront situations honestly, we are in a much better position to understand exactly what God wants us to do for Him.

Be Filled with the Spirit

The Holy Spirit is sent to guide and comfort us. Being filled with this Spirit means you open your life to Him—not just up to your waist, so it appears like you are walking with Christ. Not even up to your neck, where you heart is usually in the right place, but up to the very top of your head, so your heart, mind, and entire being are shaped toward the mind of Christ (1 Corinthians 2:16). As you grow into the mind of Christ, you begin to think like God. And when you start thinking like Him, you are more apt to discern what the specific will of God is for you. Your will begins to mesh with God's will.

Speak to Each Other with Psalms, and Make Music in Your Heart to God

You will more likely be in touch with God's will when you immerse yourself in worshiping Him. The Christian faith is a singing faith, but life with all of its trouble tries to steal the song from us. That's why an attitude of worship is so important. When you make your way through life singing praise to God, you are more likely to hear God "singing back."

Give Thanks to God for Everything

We are more likely to get in touch with the will of God when we cultivate thankful hearts. When we think about our lives in light of God's grace and our personal relationship with Christ, we should be thankful. Thankful hearts beat more closely in sync with God's heart and what He wants for us.

God's specific will is what people often think of as the "fun part." It's exciting to think that the God of the universe has a particular plan in mind for our lives. That knowledge takes immense pressure off us in determining the right course of action when we face decisions. Unlike God's general will, though, discerning His specific will usually takes discipline and focus on our part. Fortunately, there is a way to be practical in determining God's specific will for you and your company. I've developed a checklist of questions to help you discern the specific actions that will lead you to God's best in your circumstances. As you read through it, you may want to think about how each question applies to a decision you need to make right now.

1. Do any of the options I am weighing violate God's general will? If so, you can eliminate them immediately.

2. Am I committed to doing God's will in this situation? If not, stop and pray for an obedient heart. Unless you're willing to do whatever God wants you to do, you need to ask God to change your heart before doing anything else.

3. Do I truly want to serve God by my actions, more than anything else? The reward for doing so is significant: "Delight yourself in the Lord; and He will give you the desires of your heart" (Psalm 37:4 NASB).

4. Are my motives pure? Set aside self-interest so you will be able to hear the "still small voice" of God (1 Kings 19:12 KJV).

5. Is there sin in my life that is keeping my prayers for direction from being answered? According to Isaiah 59:2, your sin will keep God "hidden" from you. And if you're married, make sure you are "considerate as you live with your [spouse], and treat them with respect . . . so that nothing will hinder your prayers" (1 Peter 3:7).

6. Has God provided the power and resources to accomplish this desire? If He hasn't given you what you need to move ahead, you should stop until He does. God may be telling you not to move ahead, or He may want you to persist in asking for His blessing so you will be sure to recognize His hand at work when the time comes.

7. Has God given me peace to continue pursuing this course of action and to make the necessary decision that will achieve the results I hope for? Chronic "butterflies in your stomach," uneasiness, sleeplessness, and the like are not from God. Peace is.

While this checklist can help as you seek God's will, knowing His will isn't ultimately about checking items off a list. It's about walking daily with God and knowing Him in such a way that you recognize when He points in a specific direction. If you are not walking with God through prayer, Bible study, and engagement with a local church community and have no true commitment to follow Him, you can't expect to know the difference between His voice, your own, and that of the world. God's voice is often subtle (as far as I know, there's been just one burning bush), and we only hear whispers if we're walking close beside someone. A sign that you do, in fact, have the necessary commitment and ability to hear God is that you persist in seeking His will and include others along the way.

DISCERNING GOD'S WILL THROUGH WISE COUNSEL

Some decisions weigh more heavily on your shoulders than others. They may require wisdom you have not yet attained, information you don't know where to find, or experience you don't have under your belt. While God can choose to impart directly or miraculously the knowledge you need, He often uses other Christians for guidance. To help you make the right decisions, He pushes you toward others in the body of Christ who have the gifts and experience you require. It could be that God hasn't given you the wisdom, information, or experience for a particular decision because He has already given it to another brother or sister in your life, and He wants you to seek their counsel. Note these Scripture passages that talk about the importance of seeking godly advice:

- Proverbs 19:20—"Listen to advice and accept discipline, and at the end you will be counted among the wise." We can be tempted to rationalize a given decision, but a wise brother or sister will see through our justifications and point out the errors in our thinking. It would be foolish not to listen to them.

- Proverbs 13:10—"Pride leads to conflict; those who take advice are wise" (NLT). You must be humble enough to admit you don't have all the answers and need help. Humility is a character trait you cannot afford to be without. As Christians, we are called to humility, and there's no better way to practice humility than to admit you don't know everything and seek advice before making important decisions.

- Proverbs 24:6—"For by wise guidance you will wage war, and in abundance of counselors there is victory" (NASB). Sometimes one advisor isn't enough. There will be times when you need advice from more than one source. Imagine the president of the United States faced with the decision about whether or not to go to war. He knows that lives hang in the balance, that the decision he makes will change many peo·ple's lives. Would he dare to make such a decision after asking just one person for advice? It wouldn't be just foolish. It would be reckless.

Although you will likely never have to decide whether or not to wage war on another country, there will be times when your decisions affect the livelihood of your employees, co-workers, customers, vendors, or community. You have a responsibility to seek wise counsel. So what are the attributes of people whose advice you want? Your team of advisors should be made up of people with:

- Intimate knowledge of your specific situation

- Current, firsthand knowledge of the areas of business involved (accounting, legal, marketing, sales, etc.)

- A firm grasp of the resources available, lacking, or required for the situation

- Education in the business and strategies you want to implement

- Experience in similar situations (other CEOs, CFOs, executives, directors, etc.)

Above all other qualifications, the people you ask for counsel must be completely trustworthy, honest, and do what they say they will do. Your advisors must be knowledgeable in Scripture, and they must be submitted and obedient to the Holy Spirit. In fact, you're probably worse off with bad counsel than you are with no counsel at all. Proverbs 12:5 offers this perspective: "The plans of the righteous are just, but the advice of the wicked is deceitful."

After leaving Humana, I started Health Management Associates, and one of my key advisors was my brother and chief financial officer, Charlie. He helped keep me in line more than once, but at one particularly memorable point of decision, I had an opportunity do the very wrong thing.

A long and exhausting search turned up a chance to take on the management of another hospital, and since at that point I was spending a lot of time on site at our healthcare facilities, I was also nearly desperate to find a hospital in a location I enjoyed visiting. When I came upon an opportunity to sign a management contract for a hospital in Florida, I wanted badly for it to be a "God thing."

Since it was a community hospital, the contract decision fell to a local government official, and he explained that if I would simply make a generous "political contribution," the contract and all of its benefits would be mine. Elated at the prospect of combining business trips with deep-sea fishing expeditions, I quickly convinced myself that it would be harmless to support local politicians in their work for the community. But just to make sure, I called Charlie to get his opinion.

"Joe," Charlie said without pause after hearing the conditions for securing the contract, "If there wasn't any problem with this or question about what you have to do, why did you call me?"

I knew what he meant. Charlie's advice saved me from compromising the integrity of the business I had committed to run exclusively on biblical principles—and possibly from serious legal problems down the road—for the sake of fishing expeditions during business trips to the Florida Keys.

Ideally, you will assemble a group of advisors committed to providing ongoing assistance with your business. That way, when tough decisions need to be made, you don't have to scramble to find the right advice. I recommend that any business owner or chief executive set up his or her own Christian executive advisory council

(CEAC). The purpose of the group is to hold you and your company or organization accountable to the goal of operating according to biblical principles. Following I've outlined guidelines that help ensure CEAC fulfills its purpose.

1. The CEAC exists to improve your perspective and understanding about crucial issues facing your organization or business.

2. The council is assembled and its recommendations accessed by the company's leading executive.

3. An effective council usually consists of five to twelve people.

4. Each council member is committed to debate issues to increase understanding, not from an egotistic need to win a point or protect a parochial interest; all have foremost in mind the best interest of the company.

5. Each member is respected by and respects every other member—without exception!

6. Council members come from a range of perspectives, but each one has significant knowledge about some aspect of the organization and/or the environment in which it operates, and they are chosen on their background of success and their desire to accomplish the Christian goals of the company.

7. The CEAC includes key members of your management team but is not limited to the management team, nor is every executive automatically included in the group.

8. The council is a standing body, not an ad hoc committee assembled for a specific project.

9. The council meets regularly—at least quarterly, if that is workable for your group.

In addition to assembling your own CEAC, I encourage you to hone your own thinking by serving on similar councils for other businesses or organizations.

The mere existence of a Christian executive advisory council is not sufficient to guide you, however. As I've said before, a tool must be used correctly in order to get the job done. Seeking wise counsel is wise only when you come to the group with an open, Spirit-filled mind. If you are interested only in presenting your decision or situation review to the group in order to hear its affirmation and support and aren't prepared to hear dissenting opinions, then you really aren't seeking wisdom—you are seeking approval for what you've already decided to do. And when God reveals His specific will through Christian brothers and sisters, it would be foolishness—not wisdom—to ignore it.

Acts 27:9–21 recounts a gripping story about the consequences of not accepting advice from a godly source. On a ship bound for Rome, the Apostle Paul warns the centurion in charge that he should not allow the ship to proceed in the face of approaching winter storms. Although Paul had heard from God, "the centurion, instead of listening to what Paul said, followed the advice of the pilot and of the owner of the ship" (v. 11). Although the passengers and crew survived, the reckless venture in the midst of winter conditions in the Mediterranean Sea resulted in the loss of the ship and all its cargo. Paul reminded them of the reason for their plight: "Men, you should have taken my advice not to sail from Crete; then you would have spared yourselves this damage and loss" (v. 21).

In this biblical account, the centurion was "the man in charge." He had responsibility for the well-being of the crew, passengers, and cargo, but by not accepting the advice of God's man on board, he failed in his duty. He took counsel from the wrong people.

Have you ever accepted advice from someone who had his or her own agenda, not God's best, in mind? It likely didn't turn out so well. That's why it's crucial the people on your advisory council are not wise only in the ways of the world. In the Acts story, after all, the ship owner and pilot recommended that they sail on, but they didn't know God.

CONVERGENCE OF THE WILLS

No matter what combination of means God uses to reveal His specific will to you—prayer, circumstances, counsel from other believers—you must be willing to accept whatever it is and be diligent in pursuing the answers that come. It does you and your business no good if you make a decision to do as God leads but then don't follow through. If you don't stick with it, no one gets to see the glory of God at work.

The more you coordinate your will with God's, the more you'll come to appreciate His work in your life and business. He does have a specific plan for your business or organization and a general plan for your life and the world, and the two will not contradict each other. Together, they magnify the reality that the work you're called to do is sacred.

> Review These Relevant Scriptures:
>
> John 3:1–21
>
> Romans 12:2

SANCTIFYING YOUR WORK

> But he who received seed on the good ground is he who hears the word and understands it, who indeed bears fruit and produces: some a hundredfold, some sixty, some thirty.
>
> —Matthew 13:23 NKJV

"What are you going to let me say?"

Seated next to me at the head table, my guest speaker for the Health Management Associates Christmas banquet leaned close. He was the head of a major ministry organization he had founded, and I was a big fan of his work. That he agreed to be my keynote for our Christmas celebration was a great blessing to me.

"I don't know what you mean." I was truly confused by his question. My guest had arrived just in time for the event, so he and I hadn't had time before the dinner to discuss his presentation.

"You know what I'm talking about. What are you going to let me say to your associates?"

It registered with me that he didn't know how "Christian" his talk should be since he would be speaking at a business event.

"You can say anything you want to," I assured him.

"OK." He eyed me, sizing up the validity of my guarantee. "Are you sure?"

I smiled a little bit and nodded, realizing he didn't know the depth of my commitment to operating my business based on the Bible.

"Yes. I'm sure."

A world-class public speaker, my guest, gripped the audience from the moment he stepped to the podium. He delivered a delightful and thought-provoking experience, and then near the end of his presentation, he set the group up for a significant closing.

"I've told you all about who I am, my business background, and my education, but I haven't told you about what gave me the real strength to be successful in the business I'm in. Now, I'm going to tell you about my relationship with God."

Fifteen minutes later, a dozen of my employees came forward at the closing invitation to accept Christ. Several struggled to hold back serious tears of repentance. But if I hadn't been resolute in my determination to represent Christ through my business, that may have never happened.

YOUR WORK IS SACRED

How would you feel about joining a church where the pastor hates his job? What if he dreaded getting out of bed on Sunday morning, cringing at the thought of having to lead a worship service? How well do you think the church would fare if the head pastor felt there was little value in his job? Or what if he thought it was fine to cut corners and give less than his best? Chances are, you wouldn't want to attend, let alone join, a church struggling under such leadership. A congregation under such leadership would surely fail. You wouldn't put yourself under the leadership of someone who didn't respect the high calling of his position, would you?

The Christian leader of a company should likewise respect the high calling of his or her position. You don't have to do "church work" to carry out the will of God. Both church and secular roles are sacred. Let me explain.

Jesus was called "rabbi" many times during his three years of earthly ministry. A powerful spiritual leader, He molded His disciples into men who would ultimately spread the gospel to every part of the world. That was obviously Jesus' time of "ministry." Yet Jesus was about 30 years old when that segment of His life began. So what was He doing for the 30 years before that? Was He out of God's will? Was He marking time while waiting for His calling to take effect? Was He merely getting by working a day job as a carpenter? Were those years wasted doing something less than truly sacred work?

If only full-time work in a church, Christian organization, or missions outreach is God's work, we would also have to conclude that Jesus spent a chunk of His life doing something beneath His status as the Savior of the world. You may not have given much thought to what Jesus did—or why—during His 30 "non-ministry" years, but hopefully, you would be uncomfortable thinking that what He did was unimportant or lacking in spirituality. In fact, His example tells us something extremely significant about vocations outside of church or missions work: they are sacred too. God has a purpose for each and every believer who walks faithfully in his or her calling. Gifts vary with what we're called to do, but it is all God's work.

If you believe being in God's will is the ultimate calling of every Christian, then every minute Jesus spent as a carpenter had as much value as when He preached in the Temple, healed the sick, and washed the disciples' feet. When Jesus was on the Cross, He was doing the will of the Father as much as when He was planing a piece of wood in his carpentry shop. Two Scripture passages, in particular, capture Jesus' unwavering commitment to do what He came to earth to do, and the verses leave little doubt that He would not have wasted a second of His life on anything that didn't move forward His mission to bring the kingdom of God to earth:

> Jesus said to [the disciples], "My food is to do the will of Him who sent Me, and to finish His work."
> —John 4:34 NKJV

> For I have come down from heaven, not to do My own will, but the will of Him who sent Me.
> —John 6:38 NKJV

Jesus learned a trade in order to make a living, and this required He run His carpentry business at a profit. His daily business routine likely included calculating the cost of goods and labor, the interplay between supply and demand, competitive pricing, the potential return on His investment, and the cost to replace equipment. In all of this, we know Jesus never sinned, which means that in all the years Jesus worked as a carpenter, He never cheated a customer, was never greedy with His profit, never became slave to a lender, and never took a step in business that wasn't perfectly in God's will.

Obedience to God's will is our calling, and if that means starting a company God calls you to start or accepting an executive role in a company God calls you serve, then being obedient to that call is as sacred an act as surrendering to the international missions field. If you open your mind and heart to consider how sacred every calling actually is, you can glean remarkable lessons from Jesus that will apply to your work.

JESUS AND THE MARKETPLACE

At first glance, you may not recognize the degree to which Jesus' work as a carpenter affected His later work during the three ministry years. Many of His actions and teachings during His public ministry demonstrate His grasp of marketplace principles and the way He wants to influence the world through them. I've outlined a couple fascinating examples of how this played out.

TAX ACCOUNTANT

"What do you want me to write down as the price for your bus?"

I stared at the sales manager for the RV dealer from whom I had just agreed to buy an RV, puzzling at his question.

"Didn't we negotiate a selling price out on your lot?" Surely he wasn't planning to renege on the deal we'd just made.

Now the salesmen looked puzzled. "Well, yes, of course we did. What I want to know is the price you'd like me to show on the bill of sale."

I studied the man's face for several seconds. He didn't appear to be making a joke of any kind.

Before I could respond, he seemed to grasp why I didn't understand. He cocked his head and smiled politely. "Whatever amount I list on the invoice is the figure you'll pay sales tax on. Even though we've struck a good deal, it's a hefty sum for tax purposes. So what amount do you want me to show on the bottom line?"

"I see. You want to save me money by listing a false sales price, right?"

"Yes, sir. That's what we do for our preferred customers."

"I see." I paused, calculating the five-figure sales tax I would owe on the real price but willing to do the right thing no matter what. "Please be honest, and put down the actual amount we agreed to."

The salesman's eyes widened. "Are you sure?"

I nodded. "Yes. I'll pay what I owe in taxes—what I really owe. I believe that's what I must do in order to honor God."

To my surprise, the nearly same dialog repeated itself the following week at the DMV office when the clerk wondered why I had so obviously allowed the real sales price to be listed on the tour bus bill of sale. I wrote what was likely the largest check she received that day and left, thankful to have been able to pay "taxes to whom taxes are due" (Romans 13:7 NKJV).

According to many Bible teachers, Jesus talked more about money than any other topic, so at some point, the subject of taxes was bound to come up. Matthew 17:24–27 reflects Jesus' remarkably forthright view of taxation:

> After Jesus and his disciples arrived in Capernaum, the collectors of the two-drachma tax came to Peter and asked, "Doesn't your teacher pay the temple tax?" "Yes, he does," he replied. When Peter came into the house, Jesus was the first to speak. "What do you think, Simon?" he asked. "From whom do the kings of the earth collect duty and taxes—from their own children or from others?" "From others," Peter answered. "Then the children are exempt," Jesus said to him. "But so that we may not cause offense, go to the lake and throw out your line. Take the first fish you catch; open its mouth and you will find a four-drachma coin. Take it and give it to them for my tax and yours."

The idea of paying taxes is a source of anxiety for many (most?) of us. Yet, Jesus' approach is so matter-of-fact that we should happily apply His thinking if we want to put our minds at ease about "rendering unto Caesar." I suggest two helpful applications for this passage. The first is simple and straightforward: pay your taxes. Be subject to earthly authorities, knowing God has put them there for His purposes, regardless of whether or not you agree with their practices. Your business should be free from fear that the IRS might pay a visit.

The second application requires a step of faith: At times, God will ask you to do something that goes against conventional wisdom. Jesus gave Peter a pretty wacky way of achieving the desired outcome (fishing for tax money!), but our role as followers is not to question God's logic but rather to trust in the God who is sovereign over every fish in the sea and every coin on the earth.

Two additional Scripture passages help reinforce each of these applications:

> And Jesus answered and said unto them, "Render to Caesar the things that are Caesar's, and to God the things that are God's." And they marveled at him.
>
> —Mark 12:17 NKJV

> Trust in the LORD with all your heart and lean not on your own understanding; in all your ways submit to him, and he will make your paths straight.
>
> —Proverbs 3:5–6

Although taxes are an onerous part of business life, paying them is a necessity (see Romans 13:7). You cannot afford to let compromise open the door to Satan in any part of your company. If you do, he will take advantage of the opportunity to turn a small concession into a big deviation from God's best.

HUMAN RESOURCE MANAGER

Jesus once sponsored a massive, spur-of-the-moment picnic for more than 5,000 people. But the story isn't just about food. It demonstrated something extremely important about Jesus' understanding of people. In fact, this story is so significant that God inspired all four of the New Testament Gospel writers to include this event in their writings (Matthew 14:14–21; Mark 6:34–44; Luke 9:12–17; John 6:5–13).

As the story begins, Jesus has taken His disciples to the town of Bethsaida for a retreat. Intending to rest after a busy ministry schedule, Jesus and the disciples are overtaken by a gigantic crowd of people who want to hear more of what Jesus has to say. Rather than turn the crowd away, Jesus welcomes them and goes back into teaching mode. He speaks to them about the kingdom of God and heals those who need it.

Late in the day, the disciples want to send the people home so they can find dinner and lodging before nightfall, but Jesus wasn't finished meeting their needs. Yes, He had taught them well, but after hours together, He knew the folks in His audience would be hungry. Since there had been no advance preparations for this event, Jesus simply gathered what was available. He took five loaves of bread and two fish, gave thanks to God, and multiplied the small sampling of food so the entire crowd feasted, leaving 12 baskets of leftovers.

Again I suggest two marketplace applications for Jesus' actions in this story. The first is that Jesus valued people. He put their needs above His own. He and His disciples wanted time for rest and relaxation, but the people needed ministry from Jesus. In your world, employees come to work each day with their own struggles. If Jesus were their boss, He would take that into account and have compassion on their needs. As Philippians 2:3 reminds us: "Do nothing out of selfish ambition or vain conceit. Rather, in humility value others above yourselves."

A second application is not so much a specific application of biblical principle as it is an observation about what happened with the resources available to feed the people. Jesus started with the little that was available. Often, you have to use whatever is available to you and put it to work. Restricting your company growth to what can be achieved through reinvesting your profits, for instance, may not be the fastest way to expand, but I think it is the best way to keep from becoming slave to a lender (Proverbs 22:7). Given that "the earth is the Lord's, and everything in it" (Psalm 24:1), you will likely be amazed at how God will multiply what you have at your disposal if you let Him tell you how He wants it done.

A broader look into Scripture reveals that Jesus isn't the only one who demonstrates the value of marketplace ministry. Many of His Old Testament forebears as well as New Testament followers also emphasize the sacred nature of any honorable occupation undertaken as an expression of obedience and worship to God.

OLD (TESTAMENT) BUSINESS

Sadly, many people think of their work as drudgery. It seems like some sort of daily punishment to endure for the sake of putting food on the table. Yet, regardless of what it may feel like, work is not a penalty for sin.

Although it may be tempting to think that work resulted from the fall of man, that's not what the Bible teaches. Work was part of the good life God gave to Adam and Eve before they messed things up. Genesis 2:15 is clear on this point: "The Lord God took the man and put him in the Garden of Eden to work it and take care of it." God created us to work! It is one reflection of the image of God in us, and it underscores the truth that God gives you work as a sacred trust.

Many Old Testament saints were faithful in the work-a-day world. Let's look at a few of them.

Noah

Noah walked with God. A righteous man, he was blameless among the people of his time (Genesis 6:9). Because he was faithful in his daily life, God used Noah's skills to do a job with eternal significance for the entire world.

Abraham

Abraham grew wealthy in livestock, silver, and gold as he did what God called him to do (Genesis 13:2).

Isaac

Isaac planted crops and reaped a hundredfold because the Lord blessed him. He became rich with flocks, herds, and servants—all of which required work to acquire and maintain. God followed through on His promise to Abraham by using Isaac as the next step in the process of creating a nation (Genesis 26:12–16).

Jacob

Jacob became the overseer of all his Uncle Laban's livestock. While he was in charge, Laban's small holdings increased dramatically because of Jacob's diligence and competence, together with God's blessing (Genesis 30:29–30).

Joseph

As a young man, Joseph tended his father's flocks. A conflict erupted with his brothers, though, and they sold him to slave traders. He ended up serving as a slave to one of the Egyptian pharaoh's officials. Impressed with Joseph's hard work and abilities, his master put Joseph in charge of the entire household, and the official's house was blessed because of Joseph. Through a difficult and circuitous path, Joseph ultimately went to work directly for Pharaoh as second in command of the nation. There, God used his work to bless and preserve the Hebrew people (Genesis 41–47).

NEW (TESTAMENT) BUSINESS

God's pattern of honoring, blessing, and using the secular work and marketplace relationships of His children continues in the New Testament. The people Jesus called to follow Him were not seminary graduates in vocational ministry. They were marketplace men whose sphere of influence revolved around the business world of their day.

Simon Peter and his brother Andrew are probably the best example. They owned their own fishing boat (maybe more than one) and had business partners (James and John, who also became followers of Jesus). Jesus didn't look down on their "lowly profession" but rather saw in them the ability to "fish for men" (Luke 5:1–11). He recognized in these masters of the fishing market a potential to expand His kingdom work.

Sacred Work—Myth and Reality

Doing business God's way continues these days through men like the late Truett Cathy of Chick-fil-A (and now his son, Dan) who honor God by closing nearly 2,000 stores every Sunday, allowing their employees to worship and rest while the competition remains open for business. And men like R. G. LeTourneau who became a multimillionaire from his heavy equipment business after reversing his "tithe"—keeping 10 percent and giving away 90.

Hopefully by now, you recognize the high calling of serving as a Christian in the marketplace. Your potential for adding to and building the kingdom of God is simply different from the opportunity that ministers and missionaries have. Nevertheless, you're likely to encounter people every day who succumb to what I call the myths of marketplace Christianity. You need to be aware of them so you can fend them off—certainly to keep them out of your own thinking and quite possibly to help others catch the vision. Too many people believe:

- There is a God-ordained separation between clergy and business people.

- The church is called to operate primarily inside a building.

- People involved in business cannot be as spiritual as those serving in traditional church ministry.

- The primary role of marketplace Christians is to make money to support the "real" ministry.

None of these myths holds up when measured by Scripture. Matthew 5:14–16 (NASB) explains why:

> You are the light of the world. A city set on a hill cannot be hidden; nor does anyone light a lamp and put it under a basket, but on the lampstand, and it gives light to all who are in the house. Let your light shine before men in such a way that they may see your good works, and glorify your Father who is in heaven.

Satan is afraid Christians will fulfill their divine destiny in the marketplace and bring the kingdom of God to every nook and cranny of the world. To prevent this from happening, he spreads the lie that marketplace work is less spiritual than church work. He paints a picture of business people as inevitably materialistic and unspiritual. Yet, as a Christian in the marketplace, you are that "city on a hill"! God put you there and will use you to bring glory to Him. As I wrap up this chapter, I'll close with a personal story that destroys each of the four common myths about marketplace Christians.

THE ATHEIST WHO TAUGHT SUNDAY SCHOOL

One of my favorite employees at Health Management Associates was the guy I had hired to be my personnel director. He was incredibly knowledgeable and gifted in managing personnel. We became good friends and talked deeply about all kinds of ethical, philosophical, and theological issues. The only serious difference between us was that I was a committed Christian, and he didn't believe God existed. Yet somehow he had studied so much of the Bible that he could quote more Scripture in our conversations that I could.

He was such a people person and so eloquent that a particularly amusing incident happened while on a vacation one time with his wife. She was a Christian, so one Sunday during their travels in Texas, they visited a church. During Sunday School, her husband was so engaging and well-informed that the class asked him to come back the next Sunday and teach. He called me that week from the road just to taunt me with the idea that he, an atheist, had been invited to lead a Sunday School class.

He didn't realize that his experience working with a company committed to living out the gospel planted seeds in his heart. After about five years, he accepted a position with another company, and several years after that, he called me. We hadn't talked in many months, so his phone call was somewhat out of the blue. His news, though, was thrilling. He had received Christ as his Savior!

I don't know when I've ever been more elated at the conversion of a friend. But notice how his experience blasts the four myths I mentioned above:

- He had little or no contact with clergy of any kind, so the only personal influences on him were his wife and his colleagues at work.

- The "church" that influenced him was our company.

- He and I talked for hours about spiritual things.

- Donating money to ministry had nothing to do with his conversion. The ministry that reached him was the business itself, not an evangelical ministry organization.

In general, religious leaders have far less contact with unbelievers than marketplace Christians who interact daily with co-workers, customers, and other business associates. This is due, at least in part, to the reality that the church simply does not command the attention—or the respect—of the marketplace. So, hoping for churches to do all the ministering is a dead-end street.

As Scripture demonstrates, work is inherently sacred, since it is part of God's original best plan for mankind. And from a pragmatic standpoint, there's essentially no other way to reach deeply into the world and bring people to Christ. I believe this is a major part of what Jesus meant when He promised we would do even greater works than He did (John 14:12–15). You have the full power of heaven at your disposal to fulfill your calling in business (John 14:14 and Philippians 4:13). Fear not. Embrace your sacred call to ministry in the marketplace.

> Review These Relevant Scriptures:
>
> Psalm 24:1
>
> Proverbs 3:5–6
>
> Matthew 14:14–21; 17:24–27
>
> Mark 12:17
>
> Romans 12:2
>
> Philippians 2:3

THE FEAR FIGHT

> Serve only the LORD your God and fear him alone. Obey
> his commands, listen to his voice, and cling to him.
> —Deuteronomy 13:4 NLT

At some point in every presentation to business leaders about fear, I
tell them to repeat these two sentences out loud:

> "I will not fear failure. I will pursue God's will through
> my talents and potential with faith, hope, energy, and
> optimism."

It's both a challenge and a commitment. It's a challenge because
no matter how much you've been able to manage your fear, more
opportunities to manage it are always waiting for you. And it's
a commitment because when the time comes, it tells you how to
respond—even though a correct response is not necessarily easy to
come by. Yet reacting productively is exactly what our war against
fear is all about.

RESPONSIBLE FOR YOUR FEAR

CEOs and business owners are paid to be problem solvers. We are
paid to make decisions. We are paid to face fear.

Just like the captain of a ship, you are responsible for your company, and your crew is watching to see how you handle fearful situations. When storms roll in, they need to know their leader (not

their ship) is grounded, prepared, and resourceful. Your reaction to fear trickles down into the company and influences every employee in your organization. It is up to you to get a handle on your angst so that the trickle-down in your business is faith, not fear.

Coaching legend John Wooden, who led the UCLA men's basketball team to seven consecutive NCAA championships, knew a lot about fear. Here's how he explained his view of this potentially debilitating emotion in his book *Coach Wooden's Pyramid of Success*:

> When we needed a basket badly, the player who wanted the ball was the one I wanted to have it. For example, in my next to the last game . . . we were two points behind Louisville with only a few seconds to go. We set up a play for Richard Washington. Afterward, a reporter asked, "Why did you pick Washington?"
>
> I replied, "Because he's not afraid to make a mistake. He thinks he's a pretty good shooter—and he is—but if he misses he'll think, *Well, you can't make them all.* He won't be devastated. Therefore he's harnessed his fear."
>
> We all experience fear, anxiousness, and other intense feelings. How we handle these emotions usually defines whether we become a hero or a coward—and there is a fine line between the two.

To be sure, feeling fear is not always a bad thing. Sometimes fear is a signal that something is wrong, and as a leader, you need to take action. Yet there are many more times when fear is the enemy and will only keep you from the action you need to take.

Like Coach Wooden's "hero or coward" comment, discerning legitimate fear from needless fear is part of your job. I still chuckle when I think of one time I discovered just how real a needless fear can seem.

BACKING INTO FEAR

Trained as a surgical tech, I spent most of my military career serving at an Air Force hospital in London, and it was quite the adventure for my young wife and me—and part of the adventure was where we made our home.

Our third floor flat stayed cozy as long as we could keep the fire going in our small coal-fired stove. Central heat was not a luxury available in our part of town. Yet that didn't stop us from entertaining guests.

One chilly night, we invited another couple from the same apartment building—a GI and his wife—down for an evening of card playing. An hour into our game, a notable cool-down in the room signaled that our stove needed restoking. At the time, steam engines were still in use on England's railways, and our apartment building backed right up to a switch-engine yard. That meant there was plenty of burnable coke—small, cast-off pieces of coal discarded from the coal cars—scattered on the ground and available for harvest most any time of day or night. Nighttime harvests, though, always made me nervous. Trains weren't the only thing that assembled in the dark outside our apartment. The area also attracted gatherings of men that were never up to any good. Still, we needed heat, so I picked up the coal bucket and headed downstairs.

At the back door of the building, I stopped and peered into the dark rail yard. I turned my head and listened to the blackness. It was late enough that rail activity had mostly ceased for the night, but I could hear the ticking of an engine cooling down somewhere across the tracks.

I stepped out the back door, studying the ground as I walked slowly along the back wall. When I reached the corner, I turned toward the small storage building closer to the tracks. The ground on the far side generally offered a sizable harvest of coal pieces.

Ambient light from the upper story windows in the apartment building offered slight visibility, but a deep shadow engulfed my target pick-up area. At the storage building, I dropped to my knees and felt my way into the shadow, patting the ground with my left hand and dragging the coal bucket with my right. Several feet in, my hand touched a small pile of coke pieces.

Excellent. We'll have a warm flat again tonight, I thought.

Relieved we would be able to keep our guests comfortable, I raised from my knees and squatted. As I did, a metal tube pressed into my back. It had the unmistakable feel of a gun barrel. I froze. I hadn't sensed anybody's presence at the back of the building, yet here I was at the mercy of a potential killer. I had nothing to give a robber, so I figured my odds of survival were limited. It wouldn't be the first time a mortified soul had been discovered by the railroad tracks.

I squatted motionless, heart pounding and hairs prickling over every square inch of skin on my body. I waited for instructions. Perhaps my attacker hadn't decided yet whether to demand money or just kill me for the fun of it. After several seconds that seemed like hours, I thought of an evasive maneuver I learned in basic training. I decided to take the initiative in the situation and swing around, grab the gun barrel, and hope the surprise movement would give me an advantage in the ensuing fight.

I tightened my left hand around a lump of coal and pivoted on the balls of my feet. As my right hand grabbed the muzzle, I pitched the piece in my left at the intruder. My chunk of coal clanked in the dark against metal as I lost my balance. Instead of gaining the advantage, I fell on my back, and a bicycle crashed on top of me, the handlebar slipping out of my right hand and jabbing hard into my ribs.

I groaned at the pain in my side—and at the foolishness of my fear. I shoved the bike back into the darkness by the wall where it had been resting before I entered the shadow. As I filled the coal bucket, though, I mused over two lessons I've never forgotten. I don't remember ever being more afraid than at that moment when I thought I was about to die, and I realized how terrible fear can be. I also realized that what we fear is not always real—which means we cannot rely on our feelings of fear to tell us if we actually have something to be afraid of.

FEAR—A FORMIDABLE ENEMY

Whether the things we fear are real or only imagined, the fact that we feel fear sets us up for a fight. I'll give a nod to the idea that some fears are helpful—not crossing a busy street without looking is judicious, to say the least. Generally, though, fear is not our friend. I believe business leaders should always be on guard against it. When fear crops up, we need to know what to do. Usually that means to put up a fight because at the heart of fear is a lack of faith.

If we walk faithfully with Christ each day, we can let go of our fears. That's because our confidence in Him reminds us that He has our best interests in mind and is always present to make sure His best works out for us. Jesus said it this way: "But seek first the kingdom of God and His righteousness, and all these things will be provided for you. *Therefore* don't worry about tomorrow" (Matthew 6:33–34 HCSB, author's emphasis). God promises to provide what we need if we seek Him, and that's why we don't have to worry.

Fear and worry go hand-in-hand. When we fear what might happen in a given circumstance, we worry, and worry is one of the greatest stresses we can take upon ourselves. Unchecked fear, worry, and stress can produce serious physical ailments, including heart attacks. But fear also attacks our hearts spiritually, and God wants us to best the fear that triggers so much hurt.

The Bible tells us to "fear not" or "not be afraid" hundreds of times. So why is God so adamant about how we respond to fear? It's because of the massive downside to letting fear win. I've outlined below a list of quick facts about the danger of fear. None of it is pretty.

- FEAR IS HIGHLY CONTAGIOUS. But so is enthusiasm. Which would you rather spread through your company?

- FEAR SPREADS FASTER THAN TRUST. It can also tear down trust much faster than trust can be built. If you let fear undermine the trust factor in your organization, you have double the work to repair damage.

- FEAR MULTIPLIES RAPIDLY. The proliferation of fear can happen so fast that by the time you react, a world of hurt has already happened.

- FEAR STIMULATES A VARIETY OF NEGATIVE REACTIONS. We're talking about anger, distrust, dishonesty, procrastination, and discontentment, to name a few.

- FEAR IS IMMUNE TO SHORT-TERM FIXES AND REVERSAL. Fear becomes a patterned reaction in people—a habit. And as you know, bad habits are hard to break. Reversing the effects of fear is also hard because the broken trust it creates takes so long to rebuild.

- FEAR REAPPEARS QUICKLY AND INTENSIFIES. Fear maintenance is crucial. You have to keep working at spreading faith and enthusiasm instead of fear. Otherwise, fear will have its way again all too speedily.

- FEAR HAS MANY UNDESIRABLE SIDE EFFECTS. Fear wears people out. It saps their energy and reduces the drive to succeed. The result is lethargy, laziness, complacency, and lack of a sense of purpose.

- FEAR REDUCES YOUR CAPACITY TO THINK CLEARLY. Frightened people often freeze up. When I was collecting coal, fear froze my brain. I could only imagine a gun in my back, and the panic kept me from a more realistic assessment of my situation.

- FEAR PREVENTS YOU FROM MOVING FORWARD IN A DEAL. The "what ifs" become overwhelming when you're fraught with fear. They almost guarantee that you won't move ahead, and even if you do, you may wait so long that you lose the upside potential in your opportunity.

- FEAR CAUSES YOU TO AVOID CERTAIN PEOPLE. You may need to know what other key people are thinking, but you're afraid it may not feel good to find out. This kind of fear will always keep you from making the best decisions. You need to know the studied opinions of competent people—even if they run counter to yours.

- FEAR ROBS YOU OF SLEEP. Who hasn't laid awake at some point worrying? Yet somehow our fears in the night mushroom into worse problems than they really are. And besides, at 2:00 a.m., there's usually not much you can do to fix any problem at work, so you might as well get some rest and take care of things in the morning.

- FEAR CAN PROMPT YOU TO EAT TOO LITTLE OR TOO MUCH. Overeating or starving yourself are coping mechanisms that get you nowhere. Both lead to health problems that only make your situation worse in the long run.

- FEAR ADDS STRESS. Fear + Worry = Stress on Steroids. There's a multiplier effect when fear and worry get together.

- FEAR STEALS SELF-CONFIDENCE. Fear makes you underestimate your capabilities.

- FEAR ROBS YOU OF FAITH. Fear can cause you to think God is not capable of handling whatever faces you.

- FEAR WORKS AGAINST MOTIVATION TO SUCCEED. Vision generally collapses in the face of unchecked fear, and since working toward a great vision is highly motivating, the failure to maintain vision eradicates much of the motive for pushing ahead.

Every one of these results of fear is undesirable—and unnecessary. Fear delivers a dismal bottom line and is the main reason we hold back from completely following God's will. But we don't have to let fear deprive us of a vibrant walk with God in every area of life—including business.

KNOW YOUR ENEMY, FACE YOUR ENEMY, BEAT YOUR ENEMY

The first step in your fight against fear is to discern areas in your life and business where fear has gained the upper hand. You'll often find that your greatest fears attack you at the points of weakness and vulnerability particular to your personality and disposition. If you took one of the gift assessment tools I recommended in chapter 2, reviewing your results may help you pinpoint areas of vulnerability.

Whether or not you use a specific assessment tool, you can probably recognize in the following list the sorts of fears you are most naturally vulnerable to. Read through the list slowly, pausing briefly after each item, and consider how much that particular fear affects you. You might even want to jot down in the margin, on a separate piece of paper, or in a journal or planner which ones seem most often to attack you at a point of weakness. While any of the fears can occasionally undermine you, most of us have several we struggle with over and over. Those are the ones you want to face down. Here are some of the most common fears facing leaders today:

- failure

- inadequacy

- embarrassment

- job loss

- business loss

- rejection

- loss of control

- employee dependency

- financial challenges

- the unknown

Chances are, one or more of these fears has played a role in your decision making in the past year, month, or maybe even in the last week. At some point, if you want to experience the blessings of faithfulness in all you do, you have to stop making decisions based on earthly fears and grab on to the hope that is in Jesus Christ. You have to let faith, not fear, take over your attitudes, assumptions, and thought processes. My brother and CFO, Charlie, and I faced exactly such a fear challenge about a year after we moved Health Management Associates to Florida.

Charlie stood inside the door of my office and announced, "Joe, we are legally bankrupt."

I winced and held my right index finger to my lips. "Shhh, Charlie. Close the door." I motioned him to sit in the chair nearest my desk. "I understand that, but you and I are the only ones who know it right now. And that's all who need to know."

On his own, Charlie could never keep a secret, but he trusted my judgment. Like him, I was troubled by our dismal cash flow, but I didn't want to undermine company morale by letting anyone else know unless it became absolutely necessary. With the hospitals we acquired, we had also taken on overhead that we had not yet brought in line with our revenue growth. I knew I could fix it, but I needed some breathing room. Filing bankruptcy was my biggest fear at that moment, yet I believed we could do the necessary—if painful—cutbacks to bring our overhead under control before we would have to go bankrupt or let anyone else know it was a possibility. My brother kept his peace. By knowing that I was doing what God had called me to do, I remained at peace as well, and by God's grace, I made good on my promise to fix our situation.

In his book, *If You Want to Walk on Water, You've Got to Get Out of the Boat,* John Ortberg shows how hope in Christ overcomes the incapacitating effects of fear. He vividly describes the moment when Jesus appeared to the disciples, walking on the water:

> Put yourself in Peter's place for a moment. You have a sudden insight into what Jesus is doing—the Lord is passing by. He's inviting you to go on the adventure of your life. But at the same time, you're scared to death. What would you choose—the water or the boat?
>
> The boat is safe, secure and comfortable.
>
> On the other hand, the water is rough. The waves are high. The wind is strong. There's a storm out there. And if you get out of the boat . . . there's a good chance you might sink. . . .
>
> I believe there is something—Someone—inside us who tells us there is more to life than sitting in the boat. You were made for something more than merely avoiding failure. There is something inside you that wants to walk on the water—to leave the comfort of routine existence and abandon yourself to the high adventure of following God. . . .
>
> Your boat is whatever keeps you so comfortable that you don't want to give it up even if it's keeping you from joining Jesus on the waves.

So how do we conquer fear and join the high adventure of following God? How do we muster the confidence to step out of the boat?

Start by getting in touch with the fears, as outlined, that most readily demoralize you. Then ask God to show you His view of how fear manifests itself in your life. If there are areas of anger, frustration, doubt, mistrust, or poor decision making in your life, these can likely be attributed to fear. Be ruthless with yourself in prayer, and make sure you're open to whatever God may reveal is undermining your effectiveness. Only serious honesty can address the root cause of your fears and not just the overt symptoms. Face your enemy, and you're well on your way to winning the fight.

Once you know who you're fighting and have made the commitment to face your foe, you need to know how to fight. I've come up with a six-point strategy for battling—and winning—fear.

#1 *Claim and practice truth.*

Jesus is our model for using truth as a weapon. At the beginning of His ministry, Jesus confronted Satan in the wilderness. The devil showed Him all the kingdoms of the world and encouraged Jesus to abandon His mission of dying for our sins. Satan suggested an easier, less demanding way: "If you worship me, it will all be yours." Jesus answered, "It is written: 'Worship the Lord your God and serve Him only'" (Luke 4:7–8). The only being truly worthy of worship is God Himself, and Jesus would not compromise on that point. He threw the truth at the devil—three times, in fact—and eventually Satan gave up.

We must remember what is true because our fears are often not based on truth. Our adversary will try to undercut our faith, but we can throw truth at him to combat the fears he dishes up. Here are a few truth assurances you can use:

- Diligence pays off (Proverbs 22:29).

- If you put God first, He will provide for you (Matthew 6:33–34).

- Earth is not your ultimate home—heaven is (Matthew 6:19–21).

- Give to God first out of what you have, and He'll supply your needs (Malachi 3:8–12).

- Anxiety is needless (Luke 12:22–31).

· Only fools hold too tightly to what they've been given—put first things first (Luke 12:15–21).

#2 *Refuse to worry. Pray instead.*

If you were to pray about a situation as much as you worry about it, how might you feel differently about what you face? Whenever you start to worry or feel fear creeping in as you think about your circumstances, pray about it. Leave the burden at God's feet, and you will eliminate the worry.

#3 *Develop an appropriate reverence for God*

It's healthy to be more afraid of refusing what God asks of you than of the unknown. When you truly walk with God, you'll do anything to avoid disobeying Him and stepping out of His will—including moving ahead even when you're nervous about where you're going. Deuteronomy 13:4 (NLT) calls us to "Serve only the Lord your God and *fear* him alone. Obey his commands, listen to his voice, and cling to him" (author's emphasis). And Exodus 20:20 (TLB) reminds us: "'Don't be afraid,' Moses told them, 'for God has come in this way to show you his awesome power, so that from now on *you will be afraid to sin against him!*'" (author's emphasis). I learned much of my own reluctance to sin against God from a strong desire not to sin against my dad.

Walking home from high school one spring afternoon with a buddy of mine, my heart skipped a beat as a car I recognized all too well pulled to a stop beside us.

"Hop in, boys, and I'll give you a ride to the house." My dad's firm, cheerful voice sounded from the driver's seat.

I hoped the smoke drifting from the cigarette held close by my thigh, away from the car, wasn't obvious to my father. "No. That's OK, Dad." I tried to sound casual. "We'll just go ahead and walk."

"Don't be ridiculous. I don't get a chance to give you a ride every day."

We had no choice. I squeezed my eyes shut for an instant to mask the pain as I squeezed the cigarette out in the palm of my right hand. I would still have the blister days later.

My dad hated smoking—so much that none of us kids ever had to ask whether or not it would be OK to smoke. We knew it wouldn't. Yet he never said a word to me about the encounter that day. I still don't know if he realized I had been smoking (although I would bet that he did), but one thing is sure: I never took another puff on a cigarette. That was too close a call with disappointing my father.

#4 *Maintain a realistic view of failure.*

Failure is not the end of the world. To the contrary, it often provides the path to sensational success. Michael Jordan detailed the statistics of his basketball playing in a 1997 Nike commercial:

> I've missed more than 9,000 shots in my career. I've lost almost 300 games. Twenty-six times I've been trusted to take the game-winning shot and missed. I've failed over and over and over again in my life. And that is why I succeed.

God doesn't ask us to never fail. The perfect guide and teacher, He knows we can learn from what went wrong. But even more than that, He simply wants us to keep the faith. As Paul said, "I have fought the good fight, I have finished the race, I have kept the faith" (2 Timothy 4:7). Failure is never the worst that can happen. Not trying and remaining unfaithful is much worse.

#5 *Get more excited about the "what could be" than you are afraid of the "what ifs."*

Any time you are confronted by fear, you are likely at a stepping point for something great. So ask yourself: What could happen if you weren't afraid to carry out God's desire for you and your business? Could you end up with better procedures, better products, new markets? Could you implement practices that actually reach souls for Him? People who work with purpose take risks because they're brimming with hope for what could happen if they succeed.

#6 *Plan for success.*

There is a world of difference between worrying and planning. Worry produces anxiety while planning produces tangible steps toward a goal. Here are some guidelines to help you plan around your fear, so you can prepare to win at whatever you want to achieve:

· *Accurately assess the situation.* However, be especially careful not to compare yourself to other people. Other people are not necessarily called to do what you are called to do. Even if some have a negative opinion of you, the bottom line is that you are committed to being faithful to what God wants from you. If you stay off other people's ladders of success, you will have peace of mind.

· *Distinguish between risk and security.* Loss is always possible, but the downside may not be as bad as you anticipate it to be.

· *Determine if the danger is real or imagined.* Don't mistake a bike handle for a gun barrel.

· *Plan any short-term action steps that may be required.* When you know what to do, it builds confidence to simply get moving.

· *Determine what help is available.* Take advantage of people and resources at your disposal. Other people like having a role in a good plan.

· *Apply trust, faith, hope, and love*—every time you get afraid, in fact.

With an understanding of your enemy, a willingness to face fear, and these six strategies under your belt, you're ready to take on the fight, so don't let fear hold you back from your calling. Think of the exciting future you'll have with no fears to get in the way. It should be enough to make you want to shout these words out loud: I will not fear failure! I will pursue God's will through my talents and potential with faith, hope, energy, and optimism!

> Review These Relevant Scriptures:
>
> Exodus 20:20
>
> Matthew 6:33–34
>
> 2 Timothy 4:7

BIBLICAL DECISION-MAKING

> Where is the man who fears the Lord? God will teach
> him how to choose the best.
> —Psalm 25:12 TLB

That guy's working really hard to ignore me.

From my seat in the reception area of the hospital management company, I watched the man who was about to interview me turn the page of his *Wall Street Journal*.

Doesn't he know that I don't really need this job? At the time, I was the assistant administrator of Emory University Hospital, although I wasn't planning to do that for the rest of my life. I was under no pressure—personal or professional—to move on from there just yet. I simply wanted to explore whatever options might be open to me. On my flight from Atlanta to Nashville earlier that morning, I had rehearsed my lack of reasons to change jobs. So the intimidation game—or whatever was going on—here at the corporate headquarters annoyed me.

The senior vice president in the next office folded his newspaper, laid it flat on the desk, straightened his tie, and placed both hands on top of his *Wall Street Journal*. The man leaned back in his leather chair and stared into space, pretending (or so I thought) to ponder something significant. I saw it as just another ploy to keep me waiting a few minutes longer. Finally, he stood up, walked to the door of his office, and invited me in.

The meeting lasted half as long as the 30 minutes the guy kept me waiting, but I was more than ready to hit the road for my next interview stop. After a three-hour drive up I-65 from Nashville to Louisville, Kentucky, I was certain the Humana Corporation couldn't do any more to make me feel unappreciated.

I was right.

Because of the variables in my schedule, the appointment time in Louisville was flexible. I was still standing at the receptionist's desk at the office of the board chairman when he returned from a midafternoon tennis match. The sixtysomething man in shorts smiled enthusiastically and extended his hand.

"You're Joe, right? It's great to see you. I'm really glad you could make it here to meet us this afternoon."

I shook his hand. "Well, I'm glad too." (He didn't know how extremely glad I was that he was glad.)

He asked me to give him a few minutes to stow tennis gear in his office and then our interview could start. As he stepped away, another man in jeans, open collar shirt, and loafers with no socks walked in from the hall. The president was intending to meet with us as well.

My Humana interview lasted no longer than the meeting in Nashville. I had gone to school at Bowling Green College of Commerce with one of the corporate officers, and he had recommended me highly for the position. For several years he had been trying to get me to join him at Extendicare, the nursing home management company that would eventually become Humana. I had no interest in working with nursing homes and didn't agree to an interview at the company until my friend told me that Extendicare had just acquired six hospitals and wanted to run them as a for-profit corporation. In my mind, I was in, and after a short series of questions from the chairman of the board and president, I was evidently in with them too. Fifteen minutes after our meeting started, they placed a job offer on the table.

The quick proposal surprised me, but I was glad to feel so appreciated. However, I hadn't asked all my questions.

I leaned forward on the edge of the sofa in the chairman's sitting area and looked at the jean-clad president and then at the tennis-playing chief of everything. "First, let me ask you some things." I paused. "How much authority will I have to run these hospitals?"

The chairman's enthusiastic smile returned. "As long as you make more decisions right than wrong, you'll have all the authority you need."

Nodding, I looked at the president. "OK. How many people would I have working for me now in that part of the company?"

"None." The president nodded back. "You hire whomever you want and in whatever number you think you need."

I leaned back on the soft couch. Good decisions equal plenty of authority. Hiring decisions all mine. I liked the sound of that, and a month later, my family and I were living in Louisville, Kentucky.

DECISIONS, A FACT OF LIFE

No two days at the office are alike because business changes daily. Many people think of change as something bad. They view change as a problem. That's because we often tend to get comfortable with the status quo and wish things would just mosey along the way they are. What's more, any time change comes along, a decision is required.

In the last chapter, I pointed out that corporate officers are paid to face fear, and one of the most fearful things business leaders face is the prospect of making a wrong decision. But why focus on the downside? I have seen time and again that good decisions can change a problem or confusing situation into a golden opportunity. Making the most of these opportunities is the way businesses thrive and prosper. Opportunities make you rich, and decisions are the means to that end.

We do not make decisions in a vacuum, and God can help you manage both the internal and external factors that influence decisions. Internally, decision-making bumps into personal issues like pride and fear. Externally, we face money and time pressures. As the internal and external pressures associated with a decision increase, the potential for making the right decision decreases. Therefore, in order to make good decisions and keep conditions from degenerating, you should make decisions as close as possible to the time when action is needed.

For example, you may not want to close your company because pride won't let you, and you don't want to lay people off because you don't want to hurt them. Above all, you don't want to fail. Even though failure is a possibility with any choice we make, it is usually not a probability. Possible and probable are significantly different. If you grasp that possible is less threatening than probable, the fear-of-failure factor in decision-making is greatly reduced. Even making a decision to shut down your business can create an opportunity if it is what God is calling you to do.

Discerning God in Decisions

Success is never automatic. It is always the result of making the right decision at the right time.

All people in leadership have one thing in common: they are continually required to make decisions affecting both others and themselves. Business corporations spend hundreds of millions of dollars gathering and analyzing data in order to make the best possible decisions, and even so, things don't always turn out well. Most of us know the classic stories of major business gaffs that resulted from decisions gone wrong—think Edsel and New Coke. Yet, the likely reason we know of these failures is because they are so exceptional. Such mega-blunders are not the norm.

The big question, then, is "How does a business leader go about making the right decisions?" As with most issues in business and life, Scripture gives the answer: "Where is the man who fears the Lord? God will teach him how to choose the best" (Psalm 25:12 TLB). God wants to teach His people how to make wise decisions, but first He wants us to acknowledge Him as Lord, the One who is actually in control.

In my conferences and consultations, I've heard many people offer the excuse, "I would gladly do God's will if I could just figure it out." But God doesn't play hide-and-seek with us concerning what He wants. When someone has given the I-can't-figure-out-God's-will plea, the problem usually is that the person isn't listening to God—perhaps not even trying to hear Him. As a natural consequence, the person doesn't understand what He says. In our relationships with other people, if we're not listening, it's pretty hard to know what someone else is trying to tell us. To know God's will, you have to know the God whose will it is and pay attention to what He has to say.

Scripture provides many examples of God communicating to people. One of the best stories to highlight the principle of how we must discern God's voice comes from the Old Testament prophet Elijah. Here's how he learned to distinguish God's Spirit:

> The LORD said, "Go out and stand on the mountain in the presence of the LORD, for the LORD is about to pass by." Then a great and powerful wind tore the mountains apart and shattered the rocks before the Lord, but the LORD was not in the wind. After the wind there was an earthquake, but the LORD was not in the earthquake. After the earthquake came a fire, but the LORD was not in the fire. And after the fire came a gentle whisper.
>
> —1 Kings 19:11–12

Elijah might have expected a big, booming voice to come in wind, fire, or earthquake, but it didn't. God was in the gentle whisper. We hear that sort of voice by spending time quietly listening to the promptings of the Holy Spirit.

If you want to get better at discerning God's voice, you must orient your thinking toward His perspective. As Romans 12:2 says:

> Do not conform to the pattern of this world, but be transformed by the renewing of your mind. Then you will be able to test and approve what God's will is—his good, pleasing and perfect will.

The transformations of our minds includes the willingness to sacrifice our limited ideas about the way we think things should be done, to give up our pride, and to let go of our money and time. If you have offered yourself and anything you cling to as a sacrifice to God and have refused to be swayed by what the world tells you is the norm, then you are in a position to truly discover God's will in a given situation.

MAKING THE RIGHT CHANGES

After I took over the operation of Humana's small contingent of hospitals, the organization faced some especially daunting challenges in creating a profitable portfolio of facilities. One of the most pressing cost-control needs I identified was the level of staffing for our hospitals. We needed to have sufficient employees to handle all necessary job responsibilities but not so many that we overspent on human resources. Every business faces this balancing act, but because of patient safety and liability concerns, getting this correctly balanced is especially critical in healthcare. What I needed was a guideline to determine the optimum number of employees we should have in a given hospital based on its size.

Planning and decision-making go hand in hand because good planning consists of a series of interrelated decisions, and my plan required many decisions if we were to succeed. As I began analyzing the situation, I realized we required mountains of information if we were to make the right choices.

My team and I looked all over the United States for data or business models that could help, but we couldn't find a single company that had developed a system comparable to the kind we wanted, probably due to the fact that most other hospitals at the time were nonprofits.

My first decision involved exactly how to categorize the information we needed. Up until my initiative, staffing levels in our hospitals had been determined more or less subjectively by the department heads or doctors. I decided to look at the situation department by department at each individual hospital. My goal was to come up with an overall model for staffing levels based on the hospital patient census.

As so often happens, even the research phase involved critical decisions. Wanting to include the people closest to the process, I assigned department heads from each hospital as consultants to one another. Knowing the goal I had in mind for them, they visited each other's facilities, compared staffing plans, reviewed their current results, and together came up with what seemed to be reasonable, efficient, and potentially profitable staffing levels for each department.

The results were stunning. Not only did we come up with clear-cut guidelines applicable to any size hospital, the process itself created ownership of the plan among everyone involved. Our staffing strategy was simple: We should have no more than two employees per occupied bed. It was a remarkable step forward in efficiency. Along the way, we discovered that prior to the study most of our hospitals were operating with three employees per occupied bed, so our new plan allowed an immediate 33 percent reduction in labor costs. To implement the change, we let natural attrition reduce staff as much as possible but still had to face some difficult layoff choices. In the end, though, the level of effectiveness and profitability we achieved was the hallmark of our success in improved efficiency.

GETTING A'S IN DECISION-MAKING

I've made tens of thousands of decisions, many of them crucial to the life and health of the companies I've managed. To take the mystery out of how to consistently make good choices, I've distilled the path to good decisions into five key steps: awareness, analysis, alternatives, action, and accountability. If you follow these five directives, you'll consistently make good grades in your decision-making.

Step 1: Awareness

> As obvious as it may seem, you need to know what has to be decided. Remarkably, many decision-makers bypass this foundational step. They assume they know what decision is required, only to find out later that they misunderstood what was really needed. That's a recipe for failure—and sometimes for disaster.

> So, first and foremost, determine what decision is really on the table. To do that, pray and ask God to help you correctly diagnose the issues or problems. He will help you grasp the big picture and understand His perspective. There may be biblical principles—honesty, integrity, faithfulness, do-unto-others—that must be addressed, along with the more typical business factors regarding finances, competition, and opportunities.

> Part of this step is to determine if the problem before you is even worth solving or whether or not it can be better addressed by someone else. A Christian leader's job is to serve the work-related needs of those under him or her, and sometimes the best way to do this is to empower others to solve problems and make the related decisions

rather than doing it themselves. Moses used this approach: "The difficult cases they brought to Moses, but the simple ones they decided themselves" (Exodus 18:26).

Step 2: Analysis

"What a shame—yes, *how stupid!*—to decide before knowing the facts!" (Proverbs 18:13 TLB, author's emphasis).

Gathering and analyzing facts is an obvious step in decision-making, but it's not always straightforward. Your Step 1 discernment of the decision requirements will set you up for gathering the relevant information. Often you will find that your work in this step sets you up for ongoing, long-term feedback that facilitates future decisions. Scripture affirms this: "Any enterprise is built by wise planning, becomes strong through common sense, and profits wonderfully *by keeping abreast of the facts*" (Proverbs 24:3–4 TLB, author's emphasis). The facts you need will likely include corporate reports, situation reviews, field accounts, competitive analysis, market data, and current news, to name a few. Your analysis needs to explore the Christian principles involved in your decisions. First you must ask, what biblical issues need to be reviewed in this matter? Then, use these questions to help determine your response:

- What does the Bible say about the matter?

- What does God tell me when I pray?

- How do I remain committed to doing the will of God in this situation?

- What are my interests and desires? Are they consistent with God's?

- What counsel do I hear from godly people?

- What is God saying through the present conditions and circumstances?

This is the time to get input from an advisory board if you have one (you should). Your advisory board is a device to gain understanding about important issues facing your organization. When you have major decisions to make, you need to let your advisors review what you're doing. Most likely, they will ask questions you haven't thought about but need to. It's also the right forum in which to crash test your ideas. If you can't defend and justify to a group of advisors the decision you're about to make, then you need to back off.

Step 3: Alternatives

Your fact gathering and analysis should lead you to a variety of possible choices. Articulating the potential courses of action to yourself and to other key players is a highly desirable and productive exercise. For any given decision, you'll likely come up with more than one attractive option, and that's a good thing. You need to ferret through the possibilities and come up with the best one. Again, asking yourself and your advisors the right set of questions will help you hone the options down to the one choice that will best serve you, your company, and those who work for you. Here's the checklist:

- Do any of the potential solutions violate biblical truth or principles? (Any solution that does needs to come off your list immediately.)

- Does the solution meet the needs of those affected?

- Will key people support the implementation of this solution?

- Will the solution create other problems or have any unintended consequences?

- Will the solution help avoid future problems in this area?

· In a nutshell, what makes this solution better than others? (Ask this of each course of action under consideration; the answers can really shed light on the best alternative.)

Step 4: Action

Make the decision without delay. Once you know the facts and have discerned the best choice, get going! Delay can only undermine an otherwise good decision. Part of your job at this point is to begin implementation by delegating action steps. I will even go so far as to say that you haven't really made a decision until you implement it.

Step 5: Accountability

If you're surprised that the implementation step is not the final stage in the decision-making process, then this step is especially important for you. Many great decisions end badly because there is no follow up. You must evaluate the progress of what you've decided to put into action. This is not second-guessing. Your decision has been made and put into action, and now you need to check back with everyone involved to make sure they're still on course. Assess results and decide (again!) if any course corrections need to be made.

When you're making decisions, spend time with God—maybe even some extra time beyond your usual daily routine with Him. If you talk to Him about your decisions, He will let you know when you're ready to hear from Him. He will speak when you are ready to receive what He has to say. If you make decisions according to His will, peace is the silent coach that says you're on the right track.

MORE RIGHT THAN WRONG

Since I couldn't run six hospitals by myself, my first order of business at Humana was to hire the people I needed. The company president had assured me I had all the latitude I needed to find the right human resources, and it didn't take long for me to realize that hiring men and women who simply held master's degrees in hospital administration would not work. They were trained to run nonprofit hospitals, but I was tasked with building what would become the largest for-profit hospital company in the world. So I began to hire profit-minded men and women. I decided it was more productive to take generally trained individuals who held master's degrees in business administration and teach them about running hospitals than to change the mindset of those educated in hospital management. So I hired people with MBAs and placed them under administrators to learn the business.

Near the end of my first year managing the hospital side of Humana (we still owned the former Extendicare nursing homes), our board chairman and his wife took a trip to London. While there, his wife fell and broke her leg. She ended up in a busy hospital in downtown London.

Both the chairman and his wife were charmed by the place. The hospital overlooked London's city-center cricket grounds, and many patient rooms actually had a view of the green playing fields. It's charm also extended to the patient population. Through its reputation, the facility had become the first choice for foreigners in London who needed treatment. The hospital census was made up of people from all over the world.

Although the Humana chairman assumed the London hospital was a nonprofit operation, he was so impressed with the facility that he decided to buy it while he was "in the neighborhood." That meant I had another hospital to manage—my first one overseas. His mandate was straightforward: "Joe," he told me upon his return from England, "if you can just make this place break even, I'll be very pleased."

After several trips to London with some of my better managers, we stabilized the facility's financial situation and set it up to begin making money. Within a couple of years, it was one of Humana's most profitable hospitals.

The success of our London hospital surprised even me but not as much as the feedback I received about my work. One day while in a meeting with the regional vice presidents who handled hospital operations under me, the chairman stepped into the room. All heads were turned by the unexpected interruption from everyone's boss. He had come with a simple announcement: "Men, you now report fully to Joe. He is the new operating president of Humana."

I tried to catch my jaw before it dropped all the way to the floor. He had never mentioned this possibility to me before, so I guess I had made more decisions right than wrong.

> Review These Relevant Scriptures:
>
> Proverbs 2:9–13; 14:15; 18:13; 24:3–4
>
> 1 Kings 19:11–12
>
> Romans 12:1–2

KEEPING YOUR VISION ON COURSE

Where there is no guidance the people fall.
—Proverbs 11:14 NASB

Hired as a consultant to analyze cost inefficiencies, I saw the first hint of my client company's problem when the president walked me into his office. I paused just inside the room. My eyes drifted from floor to ceiling across an expanse of 40 feet or so. Leather furniture punctuated the space, and the occupant's taste for mahogany was more than a bit obvious. My cost analysis was already taking shape.

The president motioned me to a wingback chair in his sitting area. As we sat down, I asked, "How often do you meet with customers here in your office?"

My host cocked his head, considering his answer. "Well, I guess almost never. I rarely have occasion to bring customers here."

I nodded and pointed toward a curtained window. "And the seven Cadillacs in the executive parking spaces. Whose are those?"

"They're the company cars for our senior officers."

"I guess they use them to call on your customers?"

"No, not really. It's just one of the perks we provide for our upper management folks."

"I see." I eyed the tasteful wood grain in the coffee table, then looked at the president. "In that case, I have my first two cost-management recommendations for you." The president had called me in because he couldn't figure out why the company was operating at such a low level of profitability. "If no one but you and your staff ever see this office, then you don't need a building like this. Move to your warehouse. There's plenty of room for your corporate offices there. . . . And sell the cars. If you're not taking customers around or making sales by using them, they're a waste of your money."

It was a rough start to our meeting, but he grasped what I was saying. In addition to the high-end office and executive cars, the man had also purchased a corporate jet and wandered into shaky real estate investments. He had drifted off track and was no longer spending company money on the right things. Practices that need-lessly cost him hundreds of thousands of dollars somehow seemed to "just happen." Sadly, he had gone too far in the wrong direction and ended up losing the company. The last I heard of him, he was on his own, selling life insurance.

It's amazing how easily companies can wander astray without meaning to. That's why effective managers always make course cor-rections before problems become serious.

KEEPING YOUR VISION ON TRACK

A man or woman called to run a business to the glory of God needs to cling to the company vision. Clinging is essential because the path for any business will be rough at times. Turbulence is a natural by-product of growth and change. It is also a reason new decisions are required repeatedly.

No matter how hard you try to stay aligned with God's purpose, you will have to make corrections at times to your game plan. Even for a well-scripted football team, a winning coach will make adjustments during the game to address variations in the competition's strategy, play selection, and even the team's mindset. And regardless of how on-target the course for your business may seem, corrections will be required along the way in order to get where you want to go.

There are more variables than constants in business. Employees, the economy, market trends, competition, and a swarm of other factors change continually and often unpredictably. The difference between a vision fulfilled and a vision destroyed is often determined by how many steps you take down a misguided path before making a critical adjustment.

You can apply the decision-making skills we discussed in the last chapter to making course corrections. And to be sure the need for corrections doesn't catch you off-guard, we will look in this chapter at some of the most common areas in which businesses require change. My goal is to help you be proactive about changing course before the drift puts your vision in jeopardy.

WHEN VISION CRUMBLES

An agitated hospital administrator called me one day. "Joe," he blurted over the phone, "I don't know what to do about my top surgeon."

Any concern with a top surgeon in one of my hospitals immediately became a top priority for me. The administrator had my attention, and I encouraged him to explain the situation.

"Well, this guy loves to eat peanut butter crackers, and he wants me to let him stock them in the doctor's lounge. But I know if I do, it will make an awful mess. You know how crumbly those crackers can be! He even threatened to take his surgery business to other hospitals if I don't let him have what he wants. What do you think I ought to do?"

His question astounded me. My administrator wondered if crumbs on the break room floor were worth losing hundreds of thousands of dollars in revenue. I calmed myself, though, and answered kindly but forthrightly.

"If that doctor needs a tractor trailer load of peanut butter crackers parked at the doctor's lounge, get one there today. And I don't care how big a mountain of crumbs he leaves on the floor. If he makes a mess, clean it up yourself if you have to."

The man on the other end of the line said nothing.

"Just to be clear," I added, "your surgeon is worth the trouble."

My administrator had lost sight of the vision we shared for our hospital expertise. We provided high-quality surgical procedures (among other services) for our patients, and keeping the best surgeon we had happy was worth some extra janitorial trouble. Thankfully, my manager saw I was right, and his adjustment in thinking saved us from a serious problem. Cracker crumbs were a small price to pay for staying true to our vision of excellent service and value.

KEEP YOUR EMPLOYEES IN THE KNOW

Suppose someone walked into your business today and asked your employees: "What is the mission of this company?" or "What does this company stand for?"

How would your colleagues answer?

If employees are on board with your vision and mission, they can readily explain your company purpose. Anyone at any place in your organization should be able to tell in a sentence or two what your company is in business for. Every worker should be clear about your shared vision.

Employees with shared vision will also help you solve problems. But if you don't let them in on your purpose, they will think problems don't affect them because they have never taken ownership or pride in what you are doing together.

In *Business Proverbs: Daily Wisdom for the Workplace*, Steve Marr shares insights into the importance of making sure everyone in the workplace owns the company vision. Here are a few pithy quotes from his book that point out what you need to keep in mind:

> "Look behind you. If no one is following, you're not leading. You're just taking a walk."

> "Managers must accept the responsibility for ensuring that every team member understands the mission, visions, and direction of the company."

> "When adversity strikes your business, be open and honest with your staff. Explain the situation and communicate your resolve to find a solution together."

> "As you open up with your employees, they will open up with you and all kinds of great ideas will surface."

If you routinely communicate your vision, employees will adopt it.

Since vision starts with you and your relationship to God, your company reflects who you are. It is a natural consequence of every organization that it takes on the characteristics and personality of its leader. Hopefully, that is not a scary thought for you. If so, one of the corrections you need to make is to adjust yourself, so you're comfortable with what your organization is becoming.

When trouble arises, it is often due to poor leadership. Major companies sometimes pay gigantic amounts of money to bring in a new CEO because they know how dramatically one person can affect an organization, and a key function of good leadership is communicating the corporate mission. Scripture makes clear the importance of leaders handling this well:

You know full well the tragedy of our city; it lies in ruins and its gates are burned. Let us rebuild the wall of Jerusalem and rid ourselves of this disgrace!

—Nehemiah 2:17 TLB

(Start with a solid, invigorating vision—like rebuilding the walls of Jerusalem—and keep it in front of your people at all times.)

Where there is no guidance the people fall.

—Proverbs 11:14 NASB

(Your people need you to lead them with vision!)

Vision among your employees is imperative because what they believe about your company will influence virtually every aspect of how they work—relationships with customers, their own commitment to excellence, their loyalty to the company, and more.

EXCELLING AT SERVICE

Floridians love their pools. I know because I was one of them for many years—and still manage to be a temporary one as often as I can. So, good pool care is a high priority for most residents. Yet the companies that serve them don't always get it right.

Although I was usually at the office when my pool-cleaning company made its regular service call at the house, one eye-opening day I worked quietly at my desk by the back window when the pool cleaner stopped in to do the job. I glanced up as the woman walked past with cleaning hoses and vacuum in hand. I watched her swipe the pool bottom a time or two and then returned my attention to the papers on my desk. Seconds later, her shadow passed my window again, and I glanced up, assuming she was retrieving a hose extension or something else needed for the job. To my shock, though, she headed straight to her truck and drove off. The job certainly wasn't done, but she was.

Once I was sure the woman had no intention of returning, I called the pool company and talked to the service manager. Figuring he would be grateful for my quality control input, I was taken aback when he began to harangue me about the high quality service his company provides. Nothing I said could convince him that I had just been cheated out of a decent pool cleaning by his lackadaisical employee. Somewhere along the line, any commitment to real service by the company had given way to status quo justification of sloppy work.

Serving customers will never go out of style even though some organizations lose sight of the centrality of good customer service. Yet how refreshing is it to deal with a company that provides top-notch value? You'll go out of your way to work with a business that provides great service, won't you? In fact, you're probably willing to pay more when you know a company is completely committed to serving you with excellence.

The valuation of a company is directly proportional to the service it provides because profits do not exist without customers, and customers do not exist without good service. Extreme vigilance is critical to keeping customer service high. It should be one of the first aspects of company activity you think about every day to make sure you don't drift off course. If, like my pool service manager, you're trying to convince customers that you offer good service, then the reality is that you probably don't. If you serve well, your customers will notice.

While in school at Bowling Green College of Commerce, I noticed—and still think back on frequently—a remarkable customer service experience I encountered at a local service station. Each time I stopped for gas, the owner and chief attendant (stations were not self-service in those days) asked if he could vacuum my car for me. And most times, I was in too big a hurry to let him do it. Occasionally, though, I would stop by on my way somewhere else—even if I didn't need gas—and take him up on the vacuuming offer. He cleaned my car enthusiastically every time. And guess what? Within a few years, that master of good customer service owned a chain of successful gas stations across the Mid-South.

Good service is especially incumbent upon those of us who aspire to run our organizations based on biblical principles. As Christians, we are called to lives of service, so if our companies don't provide excellent customer service, we are not glorifying God by what we do and likely won't turn a profit in the long run. Here's a listing of several directives from the Bible about serving well:

> And whatever you do, whether in word or deed, do it all in the name of the Lord Jesus, giving thanks to God the Father through him.
> —Colossians 3:17

> And if anyone forces you to go one mile, go with him two. Give to the one who asks you, and don't turn away from the one who wants to borrow from you. You have heard that it was said, Love your neighbor and hate your enemy. But I tell you, love your enemies and pray for those who persecute you, so that you may be sons of your Father in heaven.
> —Matthew 5:41–47 HCSB

> So in everything, do to others what you would have them do to you.
> —Matthew 7:12

In his book, *Business Proverbs: Daily Wisdom for the Workplace*, Steve Marr also weighs in on this point:

> "Take time to call your customers, not only to ascertain their current level of satisfaction, but to see what new products or services they desire."

> "In today's marketplace, customers will go where their needs are being satisfied."

> "In business, your customer's needs are not always so obvious. Don't make the mistake of thinking that, just

because they aren't complaining, that they are happy and satisfied."

Many times, CEOs sit in their offices (which are too often located on the top floor or some other obscure place as far from customers as is physically possible) and decide what they think their customers want. And they'll most likely get it wrong.

Sometimes a course correction about customer service involves not just knowing how to serve them but who you're serving. I discovered this critical issue once when I didn't even know I had a lesson to learn.

My work at Humana had settled into a profitable upward trend, so I was especially perturbed when the chairman of the board suggested I hire a vice president of marketing.

Marketing? I wondered. Why do I need someone to handle marketing when we're doing all right without paying anyone to do that?

The chairman must have had something in mind, though, because he persisted. After his third prompting, I relented and set about hiring the marketing specialist I didn't need. Midmorning on the new vice president's first day on the job, he joined me in my office for a discussion of our marketing activities.

He leaned forward in his chair and looked across my desk. "Who is your customer?"

Taken aback by what I thought was absurdly obvious, I just looked at him for several seconds. I wondered what kind of simpleton I had hired.

"Our customers?" I finally said, "The patients, of course."

The new guy nodded. "OK. Now let me ask the question a different way: Who decides which hospital your patients will go to?"

My eyes widened involuntarily. I opened my mouth but wasn't sure what I was about to say. "Wow," was all I could get out.

Our corporate growth had been taking place despite the fact that I didn't even know who my customers were. The doctors who used our hospitals—not the patients—were our target market. To be sure, we needed to take good care of their patients, but physicians were the decision-makers and, hence, the customers we needed to know how to serve.

If you want to be truly customer-service oriented, you need to make sure you're focusing on the right people. No course correction evaluation is complete without a review of your target market!

HIRE POWER

Choosing the right people for positions of leadership and management is one of the most important things you will do. An interesting account in the early days of the church illustrates this point:

> In those days . . . the Hellenistic Jews among them complained against the Hebraic Jews because their widows were being overlooked in the daily distribution of food. So the Twelve gathered all the disciples together and said, "It would not be right for us to neglect the ministry of the word of God in order to wait on tables. Brothers and sisters, choose seven men from among you who are known to be full of the Spirit and wisdom. We will turn this responsibility over to them and will give our attention to prayer and the ministry of the word." This proposal pleased the whole group. They chose Stephen, a man full of faith and of the Holy Spirit; also Philip, Procorus, Nicanor, Timon, Parmenas, and Nicolas from Antioch, a convert to Judaism. They presented these men to the apostles, who prayed and laid their hands on them.
>
> —Acts 6:1–6

The original 12 disciples needed help fulfilling the mission they'd been given by Jesus, so they delegated. They chose people who were "full of the Spirit and wisdom" to help them carry out their missionary goals. You too need to make sure your managers meet the same criteria. To evaluate how well a candidate for a position attains this baseline measure, I've outlined benchmarks to keep in mind as you interview and talk with references. The person you want for the job:

- Shows honest concern for people and their needs

- Does not show favoritism

- Helps others succeed

- Exhibits an enthusiastic attitude

- Gives credit to followers

- Can be trusted to fulfill promises

- Does not use his or her position for personal gain

- Listens to instruction

- Understands that his or her success is determined by the success of those under his or her authority

- Will readily align with your vision and mission

Another way of looking at prospective candidates for leadership roles in your company is to use scriptural filters such as these:

> And the Spirit of the LORD will rest on him—the Spirit of wisdom and understanding, the Spirit of counsel and might, the Spirit of knowledge and the fear of the LORD.
>
> —Isaiah 11:2 NLT
>
> (Are the characteristics of wisdom, understanding, counsel, and empowerment by the Holy Spirit evident in the candidate's life?)

> But seek first his kingdom and his righteousness, and all these things will be given to you as well.
>
> —Matthew 6:33
>
> (Is the candidate seeking after *things* or after the *Giver* of all good things?)

One of the biggest mistakes a company makes is to not go all out in obtaining a key employee for a crucial spot. If you've gotten in trouble by cutting the hiring process short, this could be an area in serious need of course correction. At minimum, you need to adjust your hiring process to make sure you choose the right people in the future. A more difficult scenario is to correct past hiring mistakes by releasing people who aren't serving as you had hoped and finding replacements.

If we follow Jesus' example in finding critical people, we will not make the mistake of short-circuiting the process. Even with the 12 great men Jesus had in place (including Mathias, who replaced Judas the traitor), He recognized the need to add one more top-level person to His organization. He went all out to get this man. As Saul of Tarsus travelled the road to Damascus, Jesus literally knocked him to the ground and blinded him with a light from heaven (Acts 9:1–18). After introducing Himself, Jesus told Saul what he would be doing for Jesus and His church. The job description sounded fairly rough—including how much Saul would have to suffer for His name—but Jesus knew His man had the makings to be the greatest of the apostles.

Hiring good people is not the time to cut costs. Human resources are your most crucial investment, so with each hire, you should ask yourself, "What is the most I can afford to offer this person to show how much I want and need him or her?" When you cannot afford to hire the most experienced candidate, a second-best option is to hire younger employees who do not command as high a salary (yet!) but who are going to become the best. The great part of this option is that you get to train them in your ways from the start.

PRINCIPLE ADJUSTMENT

Although hiring the right individual is not the time to cut costs, managing how many people you have on staff very well might be. Here's where quality is often far better than quantity.

After Humana took over operation of a large, unprofitable hospital in Florida, my staff and I analyzed why the operation was losing money. Patient census—the average number of patients in the hospital at a given time—was consistently strong, so revenue wasn't the source of the problem. Then we analyzed human resource expenditures, applying our staffing model, and wow, did we find the cause! The hospital employee roster was bloated beyond recognition. During the cost-cutting year that followed, we reduced the staff by 300 (yes, 300) people. That's enough to entirely run a small hospital, yet every position we eliminated proved to have been superfluous. By cutting our staff to reasonable levels, we saved enough money to pay for a three-year lease on the hospital's facilities!

Somewhere along the line, the folks that ran the Florida hospital before Humana had lost sight of sound operating principles. Obviously, they had never applied a cost-efficient model for staffing, and whatever principles of profitable management they may have had at one time, they were long gone by the time I took over. Surely they didn't start out with this problem. It was a result of drifting away over time from sound operating principles.

My Florida hospital staffing experience highlights the reality that best company practices do not maintain themselves. They have to be diligently applied day in and day out. Even a good practice can erode if not managed well.

Company policies guide your operations and can need correction. Sometimes they are created in haste as a reaction to a specific situation that demands attention. In a knee-jerk reaction, we decide to do things a certain way. Or perhaps we observe similar companies and see that everyone else does it a particular way, so we assume it must be right—or at least good enough. Other times we institute policies that we know aren't perfect because we don't feel there is time or resources to come up with a better way. These seemingly insignificant decisions become the fabric of your company over time, and if you don't adjust when needed, eventually the company will look nothing like the vision God gave you.

You need to be purposeful about looking at your policy and operations manuals regularly to see if they line up with the principles of Scripture and sound business strategy. This is a good place to get your advisory board involved. Ask them to critique a specific area of your company and give feedback. You should also ask employees how they think the company is doing at achieving its mission, and solicit their suggestions for improvement.

Don't settle for less than God has for you in your company. If you're in charge, He has made it your responsibility to keep the organization aligned with Scripture and with the specific vision God has established. You're not alone, though, because He promises to help keep you on track:

> I will instruct you and teach you in the way you should go;
> I will counsel you with my loving eye on you. Do not be like
> the horse or the mule, which have no understanding but
> must be controlled by bit and bridle or they will not come
> to you.
> —Psalm 32:8 9

By directing the needed course corrections, you demonstrate that you're not just a horse or mule pulling the organization along. Rather, you're the visionary, an exciting leader people want to follow.

Review These Relevant Scriptures:

Psalm 32:8–9

Ecclesiastes 4:13

Acts 6:1–7

Colossians 3:17

Do Unto Your Employees . . .

So in everything, do to others what you would have them do to you, for this sums up the Law and the Prophets.
—Matthew 7:12

Sometimes we overspiritualize the Bible. We get so intent on drawing every pious tidbit out of a biblical story that we miss the pragmatic, common sense applications. The account of David and Goliath is a narrative I've seen people do this with. Although folks are rightly impressed with the "man after God's own heart" and his desire to serve the Lord, they often overlook one of David's key motivations for killing the big guy. As a result, they miss a solid principle about how to treat employees the right way.

As 1 Samuel 17 opens, a mega-Philistine taunts the Israelite army into shrinking from battle. When young David arrives on the scene to bring supplies to his older brothers in the army, he is not yet a soldier, but the arrogance of the giant—and the paralysis of the Israelites—angers him. Impatient with the hold-up in attacking Israel's enemy, he asks a straightforward question: "What will be done for the man who kills that Philistine and removes this disgrace from Israel?" (v. 26 HCSB). Since the king (the boss) is present, David sees an opportunity, and my perception of the young man's question is simple: "What will you pay me to kill the giant?"

The request should resonate with each of us. After all, why do people work? To get paid, of course, and David wanted compensation for doing a job. Apparently, the rewards looked pretty good to him too—"The king will make the man who kills him very rich and will give him his daughter. The king will also make the household of that man's father exempt from paying taxes in Israel" (v. 25 HCSB)—and David accepted the position of giant killer.

The biblical principles on which we should base our operations often stare us right in the face, but we miss them. You should want your company to be the best possible place to work—the envy of those who don't work there—and it starts with paying people well to do a good job.

BEST EMPLOYER, BEST EMPLOYEES

In an article by Geoff Colvin, *Fortune* magazine reports a timeless reality of making any workplace attractive to employees:

> The average American business lasts less than 20 years
> before it fails or gets bought. The 100 Best companies,
> on average, are an incredible 85 years old. Bottom line:
> Being a great place to work pays.

Sounds great, right? "Being a great place to work" may be the bar you're trying to reach, but the obvious question is: How do you become that?

Money is an obvious answer, and compensation is certainly the foundation of your relationship with employees. They work for money, so if you don't get that right, nothing else you do will keep them there. You'll recall that in the last chapter, I said not to take shortcuts on this point. Once you've hired good people on a good salary, though, there's still more you can do to make your company the best place to work.

At Humana, I introduced an opportunity for recognition called the President's Club. We used it to reward hospital administrators who achieved goals based on quality care metrics and budgetary success. At the end each year, we honored them at company headquarters by treating the winning administrators and their spouses to an extravagant weekend. It started with a lavish dinner and followed up with a breakfast for spouses and a $500 shopping spree at the best department store in town. Each administrator also received a "winner's jacket"—a sport coat featuring the company logo. You might think top managers would be most excited about the bonuses they receive each year, but we discovered that they paid much more attention to how they were tracking toward being in the President's Club than they were toward their annual bonuses—and so were their spouses!

Rewarding your top people is crucial, of course, but making life good at work is something you can do for everyone down the line. From top to bottom, the best employees want to stay with you simply if you provide a place they enjoy coming to work every day. To do that, you need to foster an environment that makes people feel significant and well cared for. You can do little things that cultivate a corporate culture in which people thrive.

Your benefits package extends beyond health insurance and vacation time. Include other perks that make people glad to be on your team. And even though many staff-friendly, people-encouraging ideas don't cost very much, they can make a big difference in an employee's attitude toward your business. From my own experience and from observing other well-run companies, I've gleaned a wide range of encouraging ideas you can implement:

- Have lunch with your employees.

- Send birthday and anniversary cards (with a Christian message) to your associates.

- Visit employees in the hospital.

- Invite co-workers to your home.

- Lead a group Bible study before work or during lunch.

- Share your faith.

- Offer to pray for a worker who shares a problem with you.

- Make job skills training available to employees.

- Ask for suggestions on how to improve company operations or employee relations.

- Know your employees' life and work desires.

- Offer praise freely.

- Provide free bagels or doughnuts once a week.

- Take staff to a movie on Friday evenings.

- Have a monthly cake day to celebrate employee birthdays.

- Have an annual "In Touch Day" where managers work your company's rank-and-file jobs.

- Develop a profit-sharing plan.

- Offer special assistance to people during their first 90 days on the job. (For the first three months, some companies provide a "new employee" sticker for their ID badge, so co-workers can lend a helping hand as needed. Then after five months, newcomers are invited to a day of skits, contests, and speakers to brush up on company culture.)

- Hold monthly breakfast meetings, and encourage your staff to ask tough questions.

- Offer scholarships or tuition reimbursement.

- Celebrate success whenever possible.

- Offer incentive bonus programs.

- Create a fund to assist workers in need, and match the donations employees make to the fund.

- Offer childcare assistance and adoption aid.

- Promote from within rather than hiring outsiders for attractive positions.

- Offer on-site amenities like massages, haircuts, dental care, even car washing and oil changes.

- Allow employees to work from home when practical.

- Offer laundry service.

- Provide package wrapping and shipping services.

- Make Christian books available for loan from a company library or for purchase at a significant discount.

- Offer to send children of employees to a Christian camp.

- Provide a company chaplain.

- Offer to send employees and their spouses to family or marriage conferences.

Ideas like these become the glue that cements loyalty among your workers and facilitates everyone's best work. Although I've been providing and encouraging small benefits for many years, early in my working life, I discovered firsthand how much a small thing could mean to an employee.

After leaving the Air Force, the next step in my career was to go back to college. I hadn't taken my studies seriously when I was fresh out of high school, but after six years in military service, I had matured enough to appreciate the value of college. So I returned to school convinced I wanted a college degree, regardless of how much study and trouble it required.

The GI Bill paid my school fees and tuition, but I had to provide income to cover living expenses for my wife and me. One of my part-time jobs—at a grocery store—provided a simple benefit that solidified my appreciation of small advantages an employer could provide. I stocked grocery shelves, and the manager told me I could take home any can of food that was missing a label. It cost the manager almost nothing because he couldn't sell the cans if the label came off in shipping or storage. To my wife and me, though, the extra food made the difference between a satisfying meal and having barely enough to eat. We didn't always know what we would be having for dinner, but the canned food was a welcome supplement to our stretched food budget.

So, look for ways to help your people. The value to them may be way more than the cost to you.

THE VISION BENEFIT

At the other end of the spectrum from little things lies one very special big thing. To attract the best employees, you have to beat dozens of competitors that a good prospect may consider. Your compensation package gets you in the game, and the caring culture of your organization keeps people with you once they're inside, but what other edge do you have in drawing—and ultimately keeping—people? The edge is the very thing we've been talking about throughout this book. Perhaps the most exceptional, alluring, and inspiring benefit you offer employees is your company vision. If you share and live out your vision, it will magnetize your organization to attract good people and keep them. I never lost a manager I wanted to keep.

People want a "why" for what they do, and vision offers people the sense of purpose they need beyond simply making money. If you implement a God-based, Christian-living vision, your company will stand out among not just dozens but hundreds of competitors.

With a sense of purpose, employees grow loyal to their company because they believe their work is worthwhile. They see, at the end of each day, that they have been part of something bigger than themselves.

While the promise of money, a royal wife, and not having to pay taxes motivated David to inquire about the giant-killing job, he no doubt also caught the vision for saving the nation of Israel from disgrace. His connection to a larger purpose gave greater meaning and satisfaction to the winning stone throw. Likewise, employees and managers sense the significance of being part of an organization committed to something meaningful—such as operating on God-honoring, biblical principles.

To reinforce the purpose your employees feel, your mission statement, guiding principles, and business philosophy should be clearly presented in a variety of ways—especially to your employees but also to your vendors and customers. When employees see your vision promoted to outsiders, it confirms the reality of what you stand for. They realize your vision is not just a motivational gimmick to get them to work hard but a driving force behind the very life of your company. This is what makes you different. This is what gives you a platform for ministry in the marketplace.

Later, I'll detail how to develop a ministry plan for your company that includes communicating your vision. A few points are so crucial to relations with your employees that I need to mention them briefly here:

- Cite your vision statement in company literature.

- Display your vision statement in your executive offices, lobby, and common areas (such as the break room).

- Remind your employees regularly about the goal, and ask for their input on how to better achieve it.

- Post your vision statement on the company website.

- Use it in your advertising—perhaps even develop a corporate image campaign specifically to promote your distinctive vision.

- Do your vision every day. (Practice what you preach!)

Corporate literature, website, and advertising are important even for employee communication because your employees notice what you say about the company to outsiders. If they see your vision featured prominently, they will more likely take it to heart.

EMPLOY A LITTLE KINDNESS

To be the best employer over the long haul, you have to work at human resource management. As with any aspect of managing a corporation, it can be done well, or it can be done poorly.

I tend to assume that most companies do an average job of managing their people—not particularly great but not so terrible, either. "It could be worse," an employee might say. Yet I'm amazed at how many companies actually do an appalling job of caring for employees. A Florida State University survey of more than 700 people working in a variety of jobs elicited a revealing set of reactions from people about how managers can treat their employees poorly. Many supervisors do not keep commitments made to their people, do not give credit appropriately, interfere in employees' personal lives, and shift blame. The study concluded that poor treatment causes low employee morale and ultimately reduces productivity.

Creating a corporate environment that fosters poor employee performance is unacceptable by any standard. It fails the standard for profitable business operations, but far more important for those of us called to operate on Christian principles, it fails God's standard for loving other people.

As Christians in the marketplace, we must pursue excellence in the way we treat people. How we handle workers is the first line of ministry, and it requires the right understanding of our positions as leaders.

Much has been made of the concept of "servant leadership," but the idea is really quite simple. The leadership positions we hold within our companies are a service to our people. Any position in an organization—janitor, assembly-line worker, plant manager—is one in which the person provides a service to the company (cleaning, assembling, overseeing). Executives and other top managers likewise provide a service.

We are servers because every organization needs leadership, and our service is to provide that for the company. Bearing in mind that we are servants—just like everyone else in the company—will help keep our egos in check and help us manage people in godly ways. We must examine our leadership practices by the measure of Scripture: "In everything, do to others what you would have them do to you, for this sums up the Law and the Prophets" (Matthew 7:12).

There are down-to-earth, walk-the-hallways methods to apply the do-unto-others principle with your employees, and I've identified seven specific benchmarks every leader should measure him- or herself by. You will do well to keep these front and center in your management practices every single day:

- Have honest concern for people and their needs.

- Actively defend the rights of your followers.

- Never show favoritism.

- Help others succeed.

- Maintain an enthusiastic attitude no matter what happens.

- Give credit freely to the people you lead.

- Be faithful to fulfill your promises.

A conscientious Christian manager implements this approach to establish trust and mutual respect with his or her employees, not just because it is good for the company but also because it is the overflow of his or her heart:

> For the mouth speaks from the overflow of the heart.
> —Matthew 12:34 HCSB

> May the Lord make your love increase and overflow for
> each other and for everyone else.
> —1 Thessalonians 3:12

Having genuine concern for people means you can't simply say you care about their needs. You have to really care. Employees can tell the difference.

In addition to the inexpensive benefits you can provide your employees, your one-on-one personal relationships with employees is beneficial too. Here are some practical examples of how to build relationships in the day-to-day work environment:

- Say "please" and "thank you."

- Be on time for meetings.

- Never use abusive language.

- Keep employees informed about pertinent company news.

- Give credit publicly for a job well done (as with a President's Club).

- Never reprimand anyone in the presence of others.

- Delegate as much meaningful work as possible.

- Restrict criticism to matters related to the job.

- Never discriminate for any reason when hiring.

- Make job descriptions clear from the start.

- Evaluate new employees after 90 days.

- Speak encouraging words routinely.

- Know your employees personally and show interest in them.

Practicing these courtesies should become a part of who you are. If you're not used to doing such things, just start, even if it feels mechanical at first. You need to turn these actions into good habits, and through ongoing application, you will become who God wants you to be for your employees.

BE A GOOD MANAGER

Courtesies and simple benefits help everyone feel better about working for you, but the managers in the next level down from wherever you are in the organization need an extra measure of trust. For them, the prescription sounds simpler than it is: You must let them manage.

All employees treasure the freedom to do their jobs as they think best, and nothing builds trust among your management team better than letting them do their share of the leading. The requirement of you is straightforward: don't do their jobs for them, and don't let them up-delegate a task back to you.

The importance of this point came home to me midway through my stint at Humana. I noticed the six vice presidents who reported to me regularly told great stories about their golf games.

When do they find time to play golf? I wondered. I assumed they used the time to discuss business issues or meet with customers, but I spent morning till night every weekday and most Saturdays in the office just trying to keep up.

Evidently, my board chairman also noticed the discrepancy between my schedule and that of my VPs because he said to me one day, "Joe, it looks to me like you work for your vice presidents instead of them working for you."

His comment triggered an aha moment that sent me back to my office to figure out how to turn the situation around. Through his observation, I realized I had allowed upward delegation to overrun my life. My management team meant no harm. Over time, they had simply come to me to discuss issues, and I went into problem-solving mode with whatever they brought me. I took on what should have been their responsibility to manage their parts of the business.

I immediately called an executive team meeting and explained the problem I had discovered. Then I returned duties and problem-solving responsibilities to each vice president, one by one. And the very next Friday afternoon, I played a round of golf. Whenever you solve a problem for your managers, you are not only doing what they were hired to do, but you are cheating them out of the opportunity to grow and gain experience.

Every manager of managers should have weekly meetings to develop and evaluate personal work plans. During the first meeting, explain the goal is to agree on specific, measurable work objectives and then determine how you as their manager can serve them in the work of accomplishing their objectives. Let them suggest what they think should be accomplished, and be sure to keep a record of the plans in order to follow up appropriately.

Your job as leader is to draw out ideas, help develop alternative action possibilities, and formulate the action plans that will allow your managers to succeed through their own efforts. This approach is extremely encouraging to those who work for you. As you start working this way, you will discover that people look forward to meeting with you. In fact, your meetings just might become the highlight of their workweek. And what's even better, you succeed when they succeed.

BE CONSISTENT WITH YOURSELF

As we wrap up this chapter, think with me for a moment about how well aligned you are (or aren't) with your intention to serve God through your business. Ask yourself this question: who sees the real you more clearly—your pastor or your employees? You are with one only a few hours a week, and then you are on your best behavior. The other you are with eight hours a day, five days a week, when you feel and act good, bad, or ugly. This is why the primary ministry of business people happens in the workplace. You're with people at work more than anyone else, with the possible exception of your family. It's critical that you become at work the person you try to be at church.

Christian managers really are the spiritual leaders of the workplace. I believe this so deeply that I think business people could start a massive revival in this country if all of us really grasped our role in God's work. People know you by the way your organization operates. That's why it's so important to make your company the best employer in the business.

As you strive to make your company the best possible place to work, your employees, customers, and vendors will all want to know how and why you do what you do. That provides an opportunity to give God the glory He deserves, and it opens a door through which you can lead many to Christ.

So, be the best employer. Your service to God depends on it.

> Review These Relevant Scriptures:
>
> Matthew 12:34b
>
> Matthew 20:25–27
>
> 1 Thessalonians 3:12

9

Managing Risk

Farmers who wait for perfect weather never plant. If they
watch every cloud, they never harvest.
                              —Ecclesiastes 11:4 NLT

"I'm going to build a grocery store out on Hillsboro Road, and it's
going to be the best one in town."

Even though I was only nine years old when I first heard my
dad describe his vision for a new business venture, I can still hear
the excitement in his voice. As I think back, I'm also amazed at my
father's faith. He didn't get much encouragement for the idea. His
bankers told him the location he had in mind was five miles too far
out of Nashville and five years ahead of its time, but Dad was not
deterred. He had heard from God and knew the grocery store—and
its location—was exactly what the Lord wanted him to do.

For my father, faith in God's plans for his life put risk in perspective. If God was in the plans, then the risk was nothing to be
afraid of. Because of the lush, pastoral spot he had chosen for the
store, my dad named his grocery business the Green Hills Market.
Ten years later, it was the largest, most profitable independent grocery store in Nashville, and now—even though the store is no longer
there—that section of town is known as Green Hills because of my
dad's store and is one of the premiere places to live, work, and shop
in all of Middle Tennessee.

Yes, Dad knew what he was doing—thanks to his ability to listen to God and take action on the message he heard. If I were to write a dedication for this chapter of my book, it would be simple:

To my dad.

(And my mother who supported him in everything!)

Although I've probably faced more risk in my career than most business people and have learned the requisite lessons, I realize that my father modeled a healthy perspective on risk that laid the foundation in my heart and soul for many challenging circumstances I faced later in life. God's direct work in my life has fulfilled what my father prepared me to do, but more than anything, Dad taught me I was always serving God first so I would know He's the main One I did not want to disappoint.

DOUBLE TROUBLE

"I really don't want to go in there," I muttered mostly to myself.

Jim glanced sideways at me and drove us past the entrance to the grocery store parking lot. I slumped against the passenger side door of our truck and leaned my head against the window. Two blocks past the store, I pointed to the customer roster in my lap and said, "Let's get the rest of these deliveries made."

After his wild success in the grocery business, my dad bought a soft drink bottling business, and now, thanks to the popularity of Double-Cola, my summer was not shaping up the way I had planned. He needed an extra delivery person for one of his busiest routes, and I became the guy.

My trouble started the previous morning when I attempted a delivery at the largest store on my delivery list. The manager met me at the back door and all but threw me out on my rear. He certainly gave me an earful of expletives I won't repeat. Nevermind that Double-Cola offered customers 12 ounces of soft drink for the same price as Coke's 6-ounce bottle. The madman claimed never to want another bottle of our drink in his store and boldly told me to go where no man would want to go.

That day, I took no for an answer from the store manager, but my father didn't.

"Doesn't want any cola!" He could hardly believe my story. "That man has been our single-biggest customer. We can't let him turn us out."

Standing next to my half-full truck of undelivered sodas, I watched silently as Dad chose his next words. After several excruciating seconds, he looked me in the eye and said, "Go back there tomorrow, and sell that man some drinks."

Tomorrow became today, and my stomach churned at the thought of seeing that manager again. The only worse thought was having to face my father at the end of the day if I didn't deliver the colas, so at 4:35 that afternoon, having been to every other store on our routing list, Jim and I pulled our truck up to the back door of Mr. Foul Mouth's grocery store.

"What the [———] are you doing back here?!" He had heard the truck pull up and stormed out the door to meet us.

I had prepped Jim on our invasion plan, and with all the calmness I could muster, I looked at the red-faced man hollering at me, then turned to my nervous helper and said, "Jim, take every last case of cola off of our truck and move it into this store."

The manager's eyes sizzled. I'm sure he couldn't believe I was serious, but Jim and I starting stacking the wooden cases of soft drinks on our dollies. Profanities erupted again as we rolled our loads past the manager, through the stocking area, and onto the customer floor of his grocery store.

"You can take those [———] drinks in there, but you'll be bringing them right back out!" He stopped his barrage of words only to catch his breath, but we stacked Double Colas in the drink aisle. We stacked them by the cash registers. We even piled cases by the door to the restroom. When we were finished, the store looked like a Double Cola exhibit.

On my last trip to the truck, I pulled out my clipboard and an invoice and wrote up my biggest order of the day, not knowing what the manager would do when I handed it to him for a signature. I breathed deeply, calming myself for the final face-off and walked back into the store where I found the man with bulging neck veins staring silently at a stack of Double Colas in his dairy department.

I handed him the clipboard. To my shock, he grabbed it, snatched a pen from his shirt pocket, scribbled his signature, and jammed the invoice back into my hand.

The exhilaration surpassed even my deepest depression earlier in the day when I returned that night and handed Dad the invoice. He was pleased (and maybe even a bit proud of his son), and I learned right then and there to always keep in mind who it is that I most want to be happy with my work.

I didn't think returning to that particular grocery store would work. I thought I would only get thrown out again, but my much wiser father knew better. He sent me there because he knew the man would buy my drinks. Although I thought the risk of failure (and potential personal injury!) was huge, Dad wouldn't have sent me if it had been a crazy thing to do. The truth is, the risk was minimal. If I had simply trusted my father's judgment, I would have known that too.

RISK—OR NOT

When we're on God's team, He wants us to win. What we think of as risks in the marketplace are only risks because we don't know the outcome of the path toward opportunity. If you want to please God more than anything else, though, you'll go where He leads and have confidence in His good will for you.

I'm not suggesting to rush headlong into any and every opportunity that seems risky. To be sure, there are times to not take a risk. The key to knowing whether or not to move ahead lies in your relationship with your heavenly Father. If you're walking with Him and have learned to recognize His voice, you will be clear on which risks to take and which not to. By spending time with God, you'll know whether or not a given course of action is one you should pursue. I've outlined below the three earmarks of a situation in which God is telling you not to go ahead.

1. *When you're not at peace.*

    Inner peace is the hallmark of being aligned with God. If you're agitated, lying awake nights, or trying to convince yourself that something is the right thing to do, then you're not at peace. Scripture promises peace in response to our earnestly asking God for direction: "Don't worry about anything, but in everything, through prayer and petition with thanksgiving, let your requests be made know to God. And the peace of God, which surpasses every thought, will guard your hearts and your minds in Christ Jesus" (Philippians 4:6–7 HCSB).

2. *When you're not at peace and your counselors say, "No."*

    There are times when good counsel can help you find peace in a situation, even if you haven't been able to arrive at it yourself. They may open your eyes to something God is doing that you hadn't recognized. On the other hand, counselors can get it wrong. If you're at peace but they say no, you might be on the right track despite what they think. My dad's bankers didn't grasp the rightness of my dad's plan to build his grocery store, but Dad had peace that God had told him what to do. However, if you aren't at peace and your counselors say no, then stop right there.

You're asking for trouble if you proceed. The risk facing you is gigantic.

3. *When your spouse says, "No."*

    You may be more business savvy than your husband or wife, but God put that person in your life for a reason. He or she is often God's mouthpiece. Sometimes a spouse has insight from God you won't get on your own. He or she can help you sidestep your overenthusiasm for a wrong direction and stay settled on God's path. At the very least, hearing no from a spouse means you should keep the lines of conversation open until both of you have peace about your decision. The time it takes to agree on the situation may very well be the extra time God needs to put the pieces in place, so your move will be right.

RISK AS GOD WOULD HAVE YOU SEE IT

I'm going to start this section with the bottom line: If God asks you to do something, He has a purpose, no matter how risky it might seem. In fact, for a man or woman walking close to God, it is more dangerous not to do something God says to do—regardless of the apparent risk—than it is to take the risk.

If you are convinced that faith in God's leading is what gives confidence in a course of action, you have won most of the battle against taking a risk. But I also want you to know the specific reasons why you can move ahead with assurance when you do what He says to do. I've identified nine specific reasons why you will be able to move ahead in peace if you are taking a risk that God is calling you to take.

1. *You will be fulfilling God's vision for your life or business.*

    Recall the promise in Jeremiah 29:11 that God has good plans for you. Stay in touch with God, and you'll hear Him speak. You may need to turn off the radio or TV, get off the computer, or be attentive when you're lying awake at night, but God will let you know what's on His mind.

2. *You know and are walking in the gifts and talents God has given you.*

    If you're feeling hemmed in and fruitless in your work but you think it's too big a risk to make a significant change, think again. God wants you to maximize the use of your gifts. Believe in Him to capitalize on your abilities, not to make you stay where you can't serve Him in the best way possible.

3. *God honors risk-taking when you do what He calls*

    In Jesus' parable of the talents (Matthew 25:14–30), two men knew exactly what their master wanted them to do, so in spite of the risks, they did what he told them to and were rewarded. The third man, though, froze with fear and wouldn't do the obvious work his master required—even though he had less to lose than the other two. As a result, what he feared most—his master's wrath—came upon him

4. *You've prayed diligently over every decision.*

    Keep the lines of communication with God wide open. Nurture your relationship every day because God can't speak to you if you don't know Him.

5. *You work at your calling with all your heart.*

    Colossians 3:23–24 (HCSB) makes this clear: "Whatever you do, do it enthusiastically, as something done for the Lord and not for men, knowing that you will receive the reward of an inheritance from the Lord." When I was a manager at Emory University Hospital in Atlanta early in my career, I met a man who demonstrated this do-it-enthusiastically principle better than most anyone I've ever known. Nothing on his resume showed any qualifications for the hospital controller position I needed to fill, but he hounded me until I finally agreed to interview him.

Thinking I would prove my point (that he wasn't qualified), at the end of the meeting, I gave him my inch-thick report on Medicare claims for the hospital and told him to figure out a better way to handle our Medicare submissions. A week later, he came back with a plan to more accurately compute our Medicare services. He had developed a method that would allow us to make more than twice the Medicare income we made the previous year! The man had convinced me that he would be an excellent controller.

6. *You are following a strategic business plan that God gave you.*

   If you've been sure to include God in your plans all along, implementing them will be a low-risk proposition.

7. *You have hired the right people.*

   If you've trusted God to lead you to the right people (or the right people to you), you will greatly increase your odds of success.

8. *You keep good records and have available the information you need to make good decisions.*

   Poor recording keeping is likely the single most-common problem I find among businesses. Maintaining bad records is a recipe for failure, but good record keeping is an incredible risk reducer. When you know where you really stand, you can analyze accurately whether or not you're in position to move in a particular direction. Often, the right choice in a difficult decision becomes obvious when you have good background information.

9. *You've financed your company mostly through your own funding.*

   Institutions or individuals who loan money take control in proportion to their investment—even if they don't know your business as well as you do. Because "the borrower is a slave to the lender" (Proverbs 22:7 HCSB), lenders take away your ability to let God lead your company. Keep control of your money, and you'll keep control of your company. Then the chances you take are between you and God—a low-risk combination.

One of our excuses for not taking risks is that we don't know how we'll come up with the resources required. Yet, God always pays for what He orders. He won't call you to do something without providing all you need (and probably more).

It's generally our choice to stay where we are, stick with the status quo, make the best of a bad situation, or settle for second best. But I'll tell you this: compared to what God wants to do with you, any of those options is a waste of life and the potential of your business. We get to choose whether to believe or to shrink back from the unknown. We decide to avoid difficult choices or to move ahead in the face of risk that really isn't risky because God is in it.

Whether sailing around the world, building a grocery store, growing a soft drink operation, or developing whatever business you are called to create, the perils can be disturbing. And isn't that great!

> Review These Relevant Scriptures:
>
> Joshua 1:9
>
> Psalm 46:1–2

SUCCESS GOD'S WAY

And we can be sure that we know him if we obey his commandments. If someone claims, "I know God," but doesn't obey God's commandments, that person is a liar and is not living in the truth. But those who obey God's word truly show how completely they love him. That is how we know we are living in him.

—1 John 2:3–5 NLT

Some people—especially Christians—seem to have mixed emotions about success. They're just not sure if being successful is godly. They wonder whether or not God will be pleased if they become rich and famous. I've seen firsthand in my own life and in the lives of people close to me the stunning things God can and will do when people succeed.

By success, I do mean financial success, but that's not all I mean. Some people who go after only money become miserable in the empty pursuit of riches. In God's hands, though, financial success can be a valuable tool for His kingdom purposes. The truth is, though, I haven't always grasped what it takes to be successful, and so I had to learn some of it the hard way.

TRAINED IN THE BASICS

High school was a daily disaster for me, but it certainly wasn't the school's fault. Duncan College Preparatory School in Nashville served some of the finest students in our community and did an excellent job of exactly what its name suggested: preparing students to excel in college. You might say, though, that I beat the system. No matter how hard they tried to teach me, I tried harder not to learn. The only part of school I cared about was sports.

Because I put all my energy into baseball, football, and basketball and cared nothing for studying, the headmaster cared little for me. By some miracle, though, I graduated with adequate grades to be accepted into the school my parents wanted me to attend: Union University in Jackson, Tennessee.

Going to college certainly was more their idea than mine, and I repeated my Duncan Prep School experience on a higher level. The larger world, though, threw a challenge at me that I was not well prepared to meet. While I attended Union University, North Korea invaded South Korea, and the United States soon entered the war on South Korea's behalf. In an effort to not attract the attention of the draft board, I enlisted in the Air Force to avoid getting into the ground fighting. I also talked a good friend into joining with me.

At the time we signed on with the Air Force, Union Station in Nashville was still a train depot, not a hotel as it is now, and that's where my journey into the military began. On our first day in the United States Armed Forces, my friend and I boarded a train for the 21-hour ride to Lackland Air Force Base in San Antonio, Texas. Neither of us knew what we were in for.

Halfway through the second of six weeks in basic training, I could hardly believe how badly the drill sergeants treated us. *How can these guys muster the energy to yell at us so early in the morning every single day?* I wondered. So at approximately 0530 on Day 10, I finally decided I'd had enough. A minute into a Sgt. Marshall's in-my-face scream over a poorly made bed, I hollered back.

"You can't talk to me that way! I'm getting the rulebook out!"

The sergeant stopped, eyes wide, skewering mine. He looked at me as if I'd just insulted his mother.

He hissed at me, barely audible, "Twenty-four hours kitchen duty."

I cringe now to think of how stupid I was to believe I could win the argument, but I didn't relent. "The rules say you have to post that on the board 24 hours in advance."

The sergeant's rigid shoulders drooped. He swayed back from his position eight inches beyond my nose, and a pleasant smile emerged on his face. "OK. We'll do that. But now you've got 48 hours of K. P. duty."

Although I satisfied myself that I had won that particular battle with Sgt. Marshall, I had absolutely lost the war. The cloud from my insolence hung over everything I did during the four weeks that followed, and I stayed in trouble, which means I stayed on the worst of assignments.

One of my missions was cleaning the latrine on a fine afternoon when the rest of my platoon enjoyed two hours of unassigned time. After roughly 45 minutes of scrubbing the bathroom floor on my hands and knees, I had made it to the seventh of about 20 stalls when a smartly uniformed soldier with gold bars on his shoulders swaggered into the room, ignoring my existence. I, however, did not ignore his.

I looked up from the tile floor and said, "Who are you?"

Surprised that I would speak to him, the man cut his eyes toward me. "What do you mean? I'm a second lieutenant officer."

"Wow!" I stared at his flawless and important-looking uniform. "Where are you going?"

"I'm on my way to the Officer's Club." He grinned slightly, amused at my lack of sophistication but beginning to have fun impressing me. "They invite women in from the community. We'll have plenty of food, a dance, shoot pool, and play Ping-Pong." He eyed my thoughtful expression as I knelt, watching him.

I blinked several times as a question formed in my mind. After a few seconds, I said, "Is that only for officers?"

The man nodded. "Yes, that's right."

Dancing, food, and games sounded pretty good to me. "How do you get to be an officer?"

He explained the process in one sentence: "You've got to go to college and get your degree."

His description of the officer track wasn't new to me. My parents as well as teachers and friends at Union had told me I should get a degree before going into the service, but their advice didn't mean a thing to me until that moment, kneeling on the bathroom floor watching another man about my age primp for a lavish night of parties I couldn't attend.

I leaned forward onto my hands and resumed scrubbing the grout from between floor tiles. The lieutenant studied himself in the mirror as I murmured, "I'm headed to college."

A few days later, I somehow secured an appointment with my company commander. Standing in front of his desk, I explained the reason for our meeting.

"Sir, if you don't mind, I've got almost four years left in the Air Force, and I'd like to resign if it's OK with you. I now realize I need to be in college. So I'm going to go back to school."

He chuckled, assuming I was introducing the real topic of conversation with a personal joke. When he noticed the serious look on my face, though, he realized I meant what I said. I think he actually felt some compassion for my naiveté, because he calmly explained my situation.

"Young man, you don't resign from the Air Force. You signed up for four years, so you're going to be in the Air Force for four years."

Looking back on my situation now, it seems elementary, but two key ingredients were missing from my life if I wanted to be successful. Until the lieutenant showed up in the bathroom that day, I had no picture in my mind of what success looked like in my life. Any thought I'd given to succeeding in life was simply that I would probably "happen into it" someday. Reality is tougher than that, of course, and without a vision for success, it's hopeless to think you'll attain it. Even if it was a rudimentary picture, seeing that officer helped me envision success. I needed to put myself in a position to succeed. Without earning a college degree, there was no way for me to achieve the status of commissioned officer in the armed forces. I needed to prepare myself for success, or it would never happen—no matter how clear a picture I might have had in my mind.

At that time in my life, I also ran afoul of several other issues God takes a dim view of. Before any of us can get on the path to success, we have to be purged of at least three basic sin issues:

- LAZINESS: Even in the Garden of Eden before the Fall, God put us on the earth to work. Adam tended the garden. If we insist on taking an easy path—like playing sports instead of studying in college—we won't succeed.

- MISUSE OF RESOURCES: God expects us to be good stewards of what He gives. He promises to set us over much if we're faithful in little things. An opportunity—like my parents sending me to an excellent university—is not meant to be squandered.

- POOR MANAGEMENT OF OUR INCOME: This is a financial corollary to the misuse of resources. Wasting money on meaningless pursuits leads to meaningless results.

THE RIGHT PICTURE OF SUCCESS

Back when I lived in Mobile, Alabama, trying to revive the ancient charity hospital there, I attended a motivational conference. The speakers were especially helpful to an upstart businessman in my shoes. All were highly successful, and all were Bible-believing Christians with impressive personal stories.

These millionaires had attained wealth beyond what most people can even imagine and had the toys and hobbies to prove it. One collected antique railroad locomotives and owned acres of land just to accommodate his collection. Another boasted several million-dollar yachts, and yet another owned one of the world's greatest collections of antique airplanes. Every one of them, though, shared at the conference that their millions of dollars and lavish hobbies left them distraught over the meaninglessness of everything until they met Jesus Christ and accepted Him as Lord and Savior. Only He offered the fulfillment and happiness they sought. He gave new meaning and direction to the use of their riches. As a result, pursuing the will of God became the driving force in their lives, not just adding to their piles of wealth.

What I first learned at that motivational conference has been confirmed for me dozens of times in the years that followed. No amount of wealth building, on its own, can satisfy the human heart, and therefore, gaining wealth can never be the true measure of success. It may be neatly quantifiable, but it's not the final answer. Just because someone has a net worth in the millions doesn't mean he or she is a success.

So if money alone is not the measure of success, what is? I've distilled the definitive description down to these eight words: success is accomplishing God's will for your life.

This definition of success is immensely freeing. It liberates us from a one-dimensional perception of success—like amassing wealth and allows us to maintain a healthy perspective on all the important aspects of life. It also has remarkably hopeful implications for everyone.

As much as I'd like to think God wants each of us to be fabulously rich, I suspect that is not His plan for everyone. I also suspect, though, that He desires many people to become wealthy who have not embraced what He wants for them. Whichever the case, with this definition of success, rich or poor no longer matters. Anyone can be a success if he or she understands God's will for his or her life and then does it. Anyone who taps into the gifts and talents God has given them and pays attention to His leading will be successful. You can be a success because you accomplish God's will in your life.

The right picture of success is the plan God has for you. To visualize what success looks like for you, you must grab hold of God's plan, and as I've said before, the main way to do that is to listen to Him. Oddly enough, many people balk at the idea. Yet I wonder, Who in the world would not want to hear directly from their Creator? I know I do, and I hope you do too. If you spend time in prayer, Scripture study, and paying attention to more experienced believers, you'll get the picture of success you need to go after.

THE READY POSITION

Once you've embraced God's vision of success, you must prepare to receive the success you aspire to. No matter how many times I might have imagined myself in an Air Force officer's uniform, I would never actually see myself in one unless I attained the prerequisite college degree. That's the way it is with each of us on the path to accomplishing God's will in our lives. We have to get in position to succeed.

Preparing to succeed starts with taking on the right mindset. I've identified three essential characteristics of a success-oriented mindset. Without them, any efforts that follow will be in vain. To get on your path to success, you must believe these truths:

- I CAN BE SUCCESSFUL. No matter what anyone else says or thinks, you must believe you can succeed.

- I AM MAKING PROGRESS TOWARD BEING SUCCESSFUL. You are the only person who can manage your success, so you need to appreciate the progress you make—large or small—along the way.

- GOD DESIRES FOR ME TO BE SUCCESSFUL. He has a plan for your life and wants the best for you. More than anyone else in the world, He has your best interests in mind.

So, if you have your image of success clearly in mind and you've adopted the right mindset, will success roll your way? While it might, the odds still aren't in your favor. To make final preparation for success, there are some practical steps you can take to maintain success readiness. I've identified 12 practical, pragmatic things you can do within yourself and in your surroundings to open the doors for success. You'll recognize them as the subjects of the 12 chapters in this book, but they bear itemizing in one place so you can have a succinct look at your steps to success as a Christian business leader.

- Establish the vision God has for you.

- Know your gifts and talents, and focus your work in those areas.

- Align your desires and goals with God's, according to His Word and your trusted advisors.

- Keep in mind that your work is sacred.

- Don't let fear control you.

- Include God in your decision-making.

- Keep your eye out for course corrections you need to make along the way—and make them.

- Make your company the best place to work by treating your employees well.

- Understand that a risk taken when God is in control is not risky.

- Believe that God wants you to succeed.

- Beware of stepping out of God's will, and set up systems to keep you in it.

- Create a business plan for your company that puts God first.

I believe God has given each of us a desire to succeed. We just need to acknowledge that desire and humbly place it in His hands. Then we can get ready to receive all that God wants to give us.

HAPPINESS, GOD'S WAY

Earlier in this chapter, I pointed out that financial success alone does not bring satisfaction or happiness, but I said that accomplishing God's will as your measure of success does. I want you to know, though, that there are specific reasons why doing God's will brings happiness. When we do God's will, He participates in life with us, and it fosters an amazing relationship between each of us and our Creator.

As you walk with God daily, the Holy Spirit will speak to you about your business. His voice is quiet but specific. You'll be amazed at how intimately He is willing to help you manage your work. I've known Him to specify my to-do lists. I end up doing things I hadn't planned but that were the most necessary accomplishments I could have done on a particular day. It's encouraging and invigorating to have such a wise, ready partner day in and day out.

Living by the Spirit also brings with it a power you wouldn't have otherwise. We access the same power Christ manifested while on earth when we make God our business partner. At times, I've felt so aware of God's leading in decisions or business strategies that I've literally felt as if I have an unfair advantage over my competition. Sometimes God speaks through specific leadings as to what to do. Other times, it comes through Scripture. If you realize the Bible speaks to all aspects of life, you can expect it to speak to your business dealings and provide answers and direction. There's no better way to have "friends in high places."

Seeing business in light of scriptural principles and listening to the Holy Spirit brings a fullness and confidence you will not find any other way. When it came to running my own business, I was convinced my company should pay vendor invoices immediately although I didn't know what the outcome would be. Trusting God, though, always has ultimately positive consequences.

As I've also said before, God wants to lead you into the fullest possible use of your gifts and talents. Countless business books have explained that people need to fit their jobs correctly in order to be satisfied in their work. Consequently, people end up regretting if they do not find work that uses their unique gifts. Few things make life feel like more of a waste than never doing what you are designed to do. But God's will always includes making the best use of your gifts and talents.

God is not only interested in how we perform at work, either. He is a well-rounded heavenly Father who wants us to enjoy the blessings of life. One of the most obvious ways I've seen this in operation was the choice God gave me of where to locate my business. When I left Humana, the obvious step for me was to start my new company right where I was—in Louisville, Kentucky. About 18 months into building Hospital Management Associates, though, I had an aha moment about where I was living. One winter day in Kentucky, it dawned on me that I didn't like cold weather. That's why Florida was (and is) my preferred vacation spot. I like everything that goes with it—sunshine, the everyday warmth, and fishing. I realized I would be happier if Health Management Associates headquarters moved to Florida. Apparently, God was glad to oblige, because the doors flew wide open—including the doors to a just-right house for my family—and I relocated the company to my favorite state.

Even God is blessed when you succeed. Now please understand that I realize God does not need anything from us to be fully blessed within Himself. He is a wholly self-sufficient Being to which we add nothing. Yet His work in the world moves forward when we succeed, and in that sense, I suggest that He is blessed by what we do. To wrap up our discussion of success, consider, for instance, the results of accomplishing God's will:

- Your business becomes a tool for witnessing to non-believers and spreading the gospel because of your financial success.

- You receive the peace of mind that comes with being a faithful servant in God's kingdom.

- Someday, God will have the opportunity to say to you, "Well done, my good and faithful servant."

- Because you know the meaning of life, you will live a life of meaning and attract others to Christ.

So, if you've ever had any doubt that success is God's plan for your life, leave it behind, and go ahead: succeed!

> Review These Relevant Scriptures:
>
> Jeremiah 1:4–5
>
> Proverbs 21:5
>
> Acts 20:24
>
> Colossians 4:2

Avoiding Unnecessary Trouble

> Spouting off before listening to the facts is both shameful and foolish.
>
> —Proverbs 18:13 NLT

Rick Bennett, my board's finance committee chairman, remained in his seat at the conference room table while nine other members of the Health Management Associates board of directors—all individuals I had come to respect and appreciate since gathering them to be my advisors after leaving Humana—sauntered into the hallway of the executive office suite. Bennett raised his right hand toward me and motioned for me to sit next to him. I set down the folder of notes I had used during the three-hour meeting that had just concluded and walked 20 feet along the mahogany table to join Rick.

I eased into the leather chair and leaned back. "Yes, Rick, what can I do for you?"

"As part of your operations report, you said you've been moving ahead with finding someone to replace you as president and take the new COO position." He paused, pursing his lips. "I'm interested."

I studied the man sitting next to me and nodded. It was true I had recognized in my ridiculously busy schedule a need to delegate day-to-day operational responsibilities. I needed a chief operating officer.

"You know, Rick, I'm not totally surprised to hear you say you're interested, but I am curious. I had planned to check with you about that possibility because Harvey McNair from SunTrust bank called yesterday. He knew the board would be meeting and suggested I ask if you wanted to explore the president's job. I said I'd bring up the idea but couldn't imagine you would really want to do it." I shook my head. "I thought you were enjoying life as a retired millionaire."

"Oh, believe me, I am. During this past year on your board, though, I've really seen the potential in Health Management Associates. So let me cut to the chase. You and I both know the most viable long-term solution to the company's chronic cash flow problem is to take it public. And as you also know, taking a corporation public is why I'm—as you said—'a retired millionaire.' When I went public with my company three years ago, they were some of the most intense but best days of my whole career. I'd do it again in a heartbeat."

"OK, Rick, you just may have yourself a job. But you know me, I need some time to pray about this first."

"Yeah, Joe, I know." He looked down and drummed the fingers of his right hand on the table. "You told us you've interviewed two excellent candidates. Don't you at least want to interview me too?"

"I just did. But let's grab lunch together next week and talk over the details. That'll give me the time I need."

"Sounds good." The board member reached in my direction.

I shook his outstretched hand. "I'll have my secretary set up lunch for us."

I nearly trotted back to my office, head spinning with the potential of bringing Rick Bennett on board as my president and chief operating officer. What could be better? He had every element of experience the job demanded—a former CEO, experience taking a start-up company public, knowledge of the pitfalls of becoming a stock-traded corporation. His demeanor even matched the corporate culture I tried so hard to maintain at Health Management Associates. And Rick already lived in Naples, Florida. Both of the other candidates would need hefty relocation packages. In most every way, he seemed to be meant for the job. *Could this be a "God thing"?* I wondered.

To confirm the "God thing," though, I committed myself to seven days of praying over whether or not to hire Rick. I spent an extra hour each day at lunchtime to specifically ask God for guidance. My prayers didn't come easily, though, and the day before my follow-up meeting with Rick, I found out why. The words God spoke to my heart couldn't have been any clearer: "Joe, don't hire him. He's not who you think he is."

I was shocked that God seemed to be leading me not to hire Rick. It bothered me so much, in fact, that I just didn't want to believe it. I wanted to hire Rick, but God said I shouldn't.

So between my last lunchtime prayer meeting with God and my lunchtime interview the next day with my board-member-turned-COO prospect, I decided what to do. I decided to take my own advice instead of God's, and the next day, I offered Rick the job.

GOD IN THE MIDST OF TROUBLES

"Smooth sailing" is never the norm in any business for very long. We may enter short periods when it seems that things move along fairly well, but bumps in the road and the need for course corrections are routinely necessary in business. With the right systems in place, you can generally take the small issues in stride. Periodically, though, your business will face major problems that, if not addressed, have the potential to sink your ship.

I find that when troubles come along, many Christians lean toward one of two unhealthy extremes in figuring out what is happening. Either they default completely to secular business practices and fail to bring God and Scripture into the problem-solving process, or they overspiritualize and take a fatalistic view of "God's will" or "demonic attack" and don't take responsibility for handling problems. Yet I believe most of our challenges are exercises God has prepared for our growth. When we stop ascribing them to the devil and start receiving them as lessons from God to be solved with His Word, we will experience His presence and power in a pragmatic new way. God is likely in your trouble for your own good.

God wants to teach you as a company leader to face problems squarely. Your list of potential problem sources includes both standard business issues as well as troubles related to biblical concerns. Let's look at the considerations in each category.

STANDARD BUSINESS ISSUES

Every business—whether run by Christians or not—has to do certain things right or the operation will simply not grow and may even fail. As a result, trouble in these areas must be addressed as soon as you recognize what's happening. For example:

- POOR RECORD KEEPING: Few issues cause businesses more problems than not keeping good records. Do you really know where you stand on key revenue and expense budgets?

- WRONG MANAGEMENT: Do you have the right people in key positions?

- LACK OF FUNDING: Is your debt-to-equity ratio off-kilter?

- LACK OF CUSTOMERS: Are you missing the market? Do you need to find new target audiences? Are you communicating effectively with the people you're trying to reach?

- COSTS OUT OF LINE: Are you spending money on the wrong things? Or are you perhaps overspending on the right things?

- BAD PLANNING: Is your typical operation to fly by seat of your pants? Do you make plans, then put them on the shelf?

- POOR PRODUCT QUALITY: Are your customers happy with your products?

- SLOPPY CUSTOMER SERVICE: Do your customers like the way you treat them, or do they just put up with you because they want what you have to offer? Do you really know your customer's needs?

- INAPPROPRIATE PRICING: Are your prices too high—or too low?

- POOR COMPETITIVENESS: Have you given ground to your competitors that you need to regain? Are you missing a competitive opportunity?

- POOR DELEGATION: Are you holding too tightly to job tasks you should give to others? Do you have managers who do that?

- LACK OF ADVISORS: Are you trying to be a lone ranger leader without getting advice or counsel from competent others?

- OUT-OF-CONTROL GROWTH: Has rapid growth stressed systems that need updating? Is this a specific source of financial pressure?

BIBLICAL CONCERNS

As you know by now, I think the most spiritual concerns are also the most practical. If you want God involved in solving your problems, you'll have to make sure you and your business are right with Him and His ways. So include these on your trouble-shooting list:

- LACK OF PRAYER: Have you made prayer for your business and the decisions you face a regular part of your routine? Do you pray about specific needs and choices?

- SIN: Do you need to repent of something in your personal or business life that's keeping you apart from God?

- LACK OF TITHING: Have you "tested God" as Malachi says and given all the tithes God is due from your work (see Malachi 3:6-12)?

- GREED: Do you have a scarcity mentality that results in greed? Do you always want more just so you're sure to have enough? Are you dissatisfied with what you have because you want bragging rights about being bigger and better than others?

- FEAR: Are you letting fear undermine your effectiveness—and your faithfulness?

- LACK OF VISION: Have you forgotten why you do what you do? Have you failed to set your sights where God wants them?

If a company goes under, is it due to sin? Not always. It could simply be poor management. You can be sure, though, that God will not bless you as a Christian if you're walking in sin or neglecting Him in some way. If you're in business with God, He wants you to succeed, and correctly handling the troubles that crop up may be His way of helping you to the top of your game.

SET UP TO TRADE

In the year after I hired Rick Bennett as my chief operating officer, he had done all I hoped the person in his position would do. I was no longer required to put out daily fires, and I ceased taking on tasks better left to the executives under me. Rick greatly eased my management role, and he encouraged my confidence that our goal of taking Health Management Associates public was realistic and could be done to my specifications.

Although an IPO promised tremendous cash benefits to Health Management Associates, I feared taking the company public would undermine my ability to continue operating it on Christian principles. No amount of cash flow could tempt me to relinquish my control of that fundamental corporate value. So each time Rick and I discussed the public offering, I made it clear: "The only way I'll take the company public is if I can continue to control it. I don't mind sharing the profits, but I want to control the company. That's the only way I can see to it that we keep operating on Christian principles."

Knowing his expertise in the private-to-public transition, Rick became my guide in the process. Even better, he confirmed over and over that meeting my one condition was not only possible but could be built into the IPO deal with lead-tight assurance. Between Rick's efficient daily management and his competent planning for our coming day of public trading, I had one of the best years of my entire career.

About 14 months into Rick's tenure as COO, we both realized the time to take the final steps had come in planning the public offering. Knowing my main concern, he explained how I would maintain control: The stock offering would specify that I would maintain control of the board of directors. As long as I had authority over the board as chairman, I could make sure Health Management Associates operated as I saw fit—biblical principles and all. The plan sounded good to me, so I instructed Rick to have our attorneys draw up the paperwork to make it happen.

Rick, along with the corporate attorney I had kept in the company when we moved from Louisville to Naples, became our core IPO team. After reviewing the stock offering documents they drew up with outside legal counsel, the plans seemed solid. My position in the soon-to-be publicly traded company was secure. I would control the board, and Health Management Associates would continue to operate to the glory of God. It looked like everything was a "go."

GETTING OVER YOUR TROUBLES

There may come a time when you think your business has come to the end of the road, but even the worst-case scenario can simply mean it's time for God to do something new in your life. Let me explain, though, how well-intentioned God is for you along the way.

If your problems are due to sin in your life—whether a moral failing in your relationships or greed and envy in your business— God would not be doing you a favor to let you continue living that way. Sin can be attractive for a season, but in the long run it always, always, always destroys us. God is into restoration and construction, not the demolition business. If you're unclear about whether or not something is eroding your business from the inside out, commit to a time of prayer and fasting to reveal the source of whatever is undermining you.

God may also be trying to protect you. Perhaps He is using a delaying tactic to keep you from moving in a hurtful direction. Someone or something may be trying to harm you, and God is your advocate in the face of danger. A lack of money to invest in a project, for instance, could be a red light warning that you should stop. At such times, it's critical to resist any temptation to take matters into your own hands and find money through excessive debt or bad deals. God is far less worried about your money problems than you are because He knows when and how to provide the resources you need. Meanwhile, He is mainly concerned about your maturity in Him. He wants you and your company to develop people and nurture honorable relationships first, and let Him bless you with profits later.

Another possible reason for trouble in your business is that you're at risk of heading off the path of biblical truth. It may not be apparent from where you stand at the moment, but God can see around the curve ahead. He knows you want to be faithful to Him, so He's making it difficult for you to proceed in a way that may cause you to deviate from His principles and hurt your relationship with Him and the people around you.

There are difficult times too when you simply need to cut your losses and move on. Don't let stubborn attachment to a failing product or outmoded process keep you in a market or trying to do business in a way that no longer works. Get on to something better!

Cutting your losses is akin to another biblical principle of pruning. Jesus said, "Every branch that bears fruit, He prunes it so that it may bear more fruit" (John 15:2 NASB). In your company, people, departments, or any branch of the business that doesn't produce the fruit you need, must be cut away to allow for healthy growth. If something in your corporation is causing you trouble because it's "dead weight," let it go.

However God wants you to get over your troubles, do what He says. No matter what combination of circumstances is bothering you, He will bring the best out of it for you.

Public Offering, Private Deal

A week before our initial public offering, my brother and CFO, Charlie, ominously appeared at the door of my office. Before he said a word, I knew he did not bring good news. Charlie was as straightforward as the accounts he had kept faithfully for Health Management Associates since the day we struggled to find our first hospital to manage. Now that we had more than 30, I respected his abilities and insights more than ever, and when I saw him so obviously stressed, my heart sank.

Charlie approached without a word. He seemed more sad than angry as he laid a thin folder of papers softly on my desk. "Joe, when was the last time you reviewed the paperwork on the offering?" Without waiting for an answer, he continued, "Have you reread all the issue paper?"

"No?" I stretched the word into a question.

"I think you ought to reread the section about your authority with the board of directors."

I nodded slightly. "Why's that?"

"Because if you move ahead with this offering under these documents, you will no longer control the board."

I considered Charlie's agonized face for several seconds. Then my eyes drifted down to the file he had laid on my desk. I reached for the documents, opened the folder, and thumbed to the section on corporate control. Charlie waited silently.

When I finished, I looked up at my brother. He simply raised his eyebrows and nodded. I reached for the phone, dialed Rick Bennett's office, and asked him to get the attorney and meet me in the conference room.

I watched them walk through the door from the executive hallway, both glancing in my direction but neither making consistent eye contact. Rick sat in the same chair from which he had asked for the president's job just over a year ago. Charlie shifted in the seat beside me and cleared his throat as the attorney took a chair next to Rick at the far end of the table. Overhead lights glistened on the shiny surface between us.

I placed my right hand on the file folder in front of me and peered at the two men at the other end of the table. "Who changed the section on the stock? And the section about control of the board? It's not what we agreed to."

The president and the attorney leaned forward, chests pressing the table's edge. "We did." Their simultaneous affirmation would have been comical under less stressful conditions.

"Joe," Rick continued, now staring me down. "That's the way it's going to be. If you try to stop us, we'll take you to court."

I drew one, gut-wrenching conclusion from the clarity of their position. From the start, the two men facing me had conspired to undermine my standing in a publicly traded Health Management

Associates. The deceit stunned me. We were due in New York in two days to make final preparations for the initial public offering. There was obviously nothing more to be said. I would take it up at the negotiations.

Rick and I didn't speak again until our meeting in New York. During the first hour, the assembled executives and lawyers, including my personal attorney, Mike, reviewed and agreed on all aspects of the offering except the disposition of my shares and control of the board. Eleven hours and four pots of coffee later, we still had not agreed on those two items. Just before sunrise the next day, I raised my hand toward the dozen or so men around the table and asked them to excuse Mike and me for a conference in the hallway.

In the corridor, I pressed my back against the wall and stared up at the ceiling panels. "OK, Mike. What are my choices?"

My longtime friend and legal consultant slipped his hands in the pockets of his trousers and looked at the carpeted floor. After several seconds, he shook his head and stared down the empty hallway.

"Joe, you can fight it." He pointed at the conference room. "Fight them. It will take you a couple of years in court and will tear up the company because of the infighting, but you'll win. You will win."

"Or?"

"Or, Joe, you can come out of the company."

Come out of the company, I thought. *The company I built. The company God led me to start for Him. Wow.*

We stood quietly together for nearly a minute.

"OK." I nodded at Mike and stood up straight. "I'll come out. I'm not going to spend two years in court."

Smug eyes followed Mike and me as we walked to our seats at the conference room table. I stood behind my chair and announced my decision to the group. After I finished, Rick spoke first.

"We need to buy your stock, and we need your name to take the company public."

I shook my head. "No. No way. My name is not to be used in any of the documents or in any promotion of the offering." I scanned the faces watching me. "And you'll pay the price I tell you for my stock."

A week later, the deal was done. Health Management Associates leapt onto the New York Stock Exchange and rewarded the early takers—but none more than me. Although the settlement group had paid my price, the final outcome still left me dumbfounded. The multimillion-dollar company I had built from scratch was no longer mine.

Review These Relevant Scriptures:

Proverbs 23:23

Proverbs 27:23–24

Developing a Ministry Plan for Your Company

> But don't begin until you count the cost. For who would begin construction of a building without first calculating the cost to see if there is enough money to finish it?
>
> —Luke 14:28 NLT

I had left for the New York IPO meetings as chairman and CEO of Health Management Associates. When I returned the following week, I was unemployed. Crushed at the news of what had happened, my executive assistant also chose unemployment rather than to go to work for the man who had ousted me from the company—even though he offered to double her salary. My administrative assistant never wavered in her loyalty to me. It was a natural part of that great lady's fine character, honed nearly to perfection once she allowed the Holy Spirit access to her heart.

I had hired her while Health Management Associates was still in Louisville, and the Detroit native relished the assignment when I told her to research the weather in Florida and find the state's warmest city as the new home for Health Management Associates. She discovered Naples, Florida, and we moved south.

Although a remarkable assistant from day one, she was not a Christian when she first came to work for me. Monday mornings brought out my compassionate side as I watched her struggle to recover from a weekend of "a bit too much fun." During our first year in Florida, though, the long-term effect of daily encountering Christian principles at work, combined with some gentle discipleship from her boss, brought her to a point of commitment to Christ. She quickly became one of the most devoted believers I have ever known, and in the years since leaving Health Management Associates, has developed a reputation as one of the finest businesswomen in South Florida.

After losing Health Management Associates to Rick Bennett, I stayed in Naples, but the proximity to my old company headquarters proved too painful. Research again pinpointed the right place to relocate our now two-person business (my assistant and me) as well as my family. We settled on Captiva Island, 60 miles north of Naples and just off the coast from Fort Myers. There, as the numbness of my loss began to wear off, I slowly opened my eyes to the possibility that God still had a purpose for me.

Before Your Plan Is a Plan

No business has any business becoming a business without a God-ordained purpose. The whole of human history has been planned by God from before creation, and you and your business have a role to play in that great arrangement. Any business plan you create will determine how you implement the purpose you have been created for and will influence the lives of all those who go with you along the way.

Unfortunately, many businesses start with little or no planning and continue to run that way—at least for a while. Others create empty plans because they fail to do the necessary groundwork. A friend of mine, for instance, once started a business with his brother-in-law. He came to me for start-up advice, and I recommended he first answer these questions:

- Who is going to make final decisions if just the two of you are in charge?

- Who will be the president?

- How are you going to pay yourselves?

- What is the legal structure of the company?

The questions seemed fairly straightforward to me—even fairly basic, you might say—but my friend didn't want to answer them. He didn't seem to think it necessary in his particular case. He and his brother-in-law, whom he claimed as one of his best friends, wanted to build the company on the strength of their current relationship and not have to define things so strictly. Ten months later, their company had gone under, both families had lost all of their savings, and the two men no longer had any contact with each other as a result of their nasty lawsuit. Sadly, I had seen their business idea and am confident that if they had taken time on the front end to create a comprehensive business plan, they would not have failed and would still be friends today.

If you operate your company without a well thought out business plan, you are running it by the seat of your pants, and I think it's odd that anyone would take such a needless risk with their livelihood. Few people operate plan-less in other areas of life. We plan to buy a house, who to marry, where to go on vacation, how much to save for retirement, so why would someone operate without a plan in business?

As you prepare to write a business plan (or rewrite your current plan) based on biblical principles, vision is the essential first element. The blueprint for your company will be the road map to accomplishing your God-given vision. That means you have to know where you are headed in order to determine the best route to get there. If you don't grasp God's vision, you won't be able to design a business that does what He requires of you.

I once surveyed a group of Christian executives and discovered that 75 percent of them could not articulate God's specific vision for them in business. So if you don't know His vision for you yet, you aren't alone. But don't remain among the ignorant! Seeking Him and His vision for you is the first step in planning. Once you understand His vision, putting a business plan together becomes much easier.

Let's quickly review the key factors you must take into account before writing your business plan. These four points are critical:

- Recognize that God has a plan for your life.
  (Jeremiah 1:4–5; 29:11)

- Give God control over your will.
  (Romans 12:1–2; Galatians 2:20)

- Recognize that God is working within you to give you the desire and power to accomplish His plans.
  (Psalm 37:4)

- Act on those desires, and watch for the power and resources to achieve them.
  (Philippians 2:13)

When you pursue God's vision, you set yourself up for success, and your plan charts the way. Strangely, though, many Christians think that creating plans is not biblical. They wrongly believe that planning thwarts the Holy Spirit. They think we should leave Him "free" to tell us what to do as we go. People think an open-ended strategy is more in line with what it means to walk in faith. I strongly disagree, though, and so does the Bible.

Scripture extols the virtue of thinking ahead, anticipating problems and opportunities, and analyzing the best ways to accomplish your goals. The Old Testament Book of Proverbs by itself is likely one of the best planning guides ever written. Here are a few samples of what it has to say about good planning:

> Every prudent man acts with knowledge, but a fool displays folly.
> —Proverbs 13:16 NASB

> The wisdom of the prudent is to understand his way, but the folly of fools is deceit. . . . The simple believes every word, but the prudent considers well his steps.
> —Proverbs 14:8–15 NKJV

> Plans fail for lack of counsel, but with many advisers they succeed.
> —Proverbs 15:22

> A man's heart plans his way, but the LORD determines his steps.
> —Proverbs 16:9 HCSB

> Listen to counsel and receive instruction so that you may be wise later in life.
> —Proverbs 19:20 HCSB

> Make plans by seeking advice; make war by obtaining guidance.
> —Proverbs 20:18 ISV

> A prudent man sees danger and hides himself, but the simple go on, and suffer for it.
> —Proverbs 22:3 RSV

> By wisdom a house is built, and through understanding it is established; through knowledge its rooms are filled with rare and beautiful treasures.
> —Proverbs 24:3–4

> Be sure you know the condition of your flocks, give
> careful attention to your herds; for riches do not endure
> forever, and a crown is not secure for all generations.
> —Proverbs 27:23–24

If you already have a business plan, then I don't need to convince you that you need one. However, the plan you have in place may not be the plan you need. If you created it without specifically trying to discern God's will for you and your business, then you absolutely need a new one. If you're not quite sure what to think of your current business plan, then ask yourself these questions:

- *What is the status of my business plan?* The most critical issue with regard to your plan is whether or not you created it with God's vision for your business foremost in mind.

- *How long ago was the business plan created?* Everything gets out of date. If you haven't gone through the top-to-bottom planning exercise in the past few years—certainly if it's been five or more years—it's time for a review and renovation of your plans.

- *How detailed is my business plan?* Generalities won't take you where you want to go. Accomplishing your vision is made up of specific steps along the way. If you don't know what those steps are, you won't get where you want to go.

- *Who prepared my business plan?* This is one place where delegation is not good. If you let someone else plan your business, stop right now and write your own plan. It's your business that you want to do God's way, so the plan must be yours.

- *How was God involved in the preparation?* If little or none, craft a new plan that includes Him in every way possible.

- *Who reviewed it?* Your advisors should be intimately involved in assessing your plans. If they weren't, at least have them take a look at the plans now and give whatever input they think you need.

LET THE PLANNING BEGIN

As you pick up your pen or sit down at your computer to write your business plan, remember who you're in business with. The Lord doesn't think small, so you shouldn't either. You'll need to be specific in outlining how you are going to accomplish your plans, but the starting point for operating on biblical principles is to have "the mind of Christ." These guiding principles will insure you follow God's wisdom rather than the world's:

- Always put God first.

- Get to know God's Word and apply it (knowing and doing are two different things).

- Expect big things from a big God.

- Place more value in people than in products.

- Tithe your company's earnings—give God the firstfruits of your profits.

- Be committed to honesty and integrity.

- Be diligent in your pursuit of business success.

- Keep good records.

- Select the right key people.

- Lead like Jesus with servant leadership as your standard operating procedure.

If you've never written a business plan before, you may wonder what to include in it. The details are easy to find online, so I will not focus on them here. Simply search "business plan template" and pick an option that looks good to you. My goal here is to make sure your relationship with God and a commitment to operate on biblical principles are central to your plan. With that in mind, there are certain traits that the business plan of a company operating on Christian principles should have.

As you proceed, bear in mind that a good business plan is one with a reasonable chance of achievement, and it must include vision and enough practical components to energize the people involved. Through the years, I've discerned a number of elements necessary to position a business for success. If you keep these elements foremost in mind and let them guide your planning, you will be successful—God's way. Your plan should include the following elements.

1. Pray through what God wants for your business and then fix in your mind the exact goals you believe God would have you achieve.

2. Determine exactly how much of yourself—time, money, and other resources—you are willing to give and how many sacrifices you are willing to make to achieve the desires God has given you. God will not honor the work of a person who wants something for nothing. Some people wrongly think that waiting on the Lord means doing nothing and having the faith that God will take care of it all. To the contrary, here's a better definition of faith: doing everything I can do and trusting God to do what I cannot do. God can do what I cannot do, but He will not do what I can do if I refuse to do it.

3. Establish a definite date by which you intend to achieve the goals God has given you. "Someday" or "sooner rather than later" are not actionable, measurable time objectives. Use your calendar. That's what it's for.

4. Create a definite plan for carrying out your desire, and begin at once. Even if you haven't figured out every step between point A and B, you can at least determine the first one or two. Sometimes you just have to get going in order to know the precise next steps.

5. Write out a clear, concise statement of the goals you intend to acquire. "Getting a lot of customers" is not a real goal. Your goal statements should include numbers.

6. Read your written goal statement out loud twice every day—once when you get up in the morning and again before retiring at night. This will make the goals an integral part of your life. You conform your mind to the things you intend to accomplish.

7. Review the plan with all of your significant advisors—spouse, partners, board of directors, advisory board, managers—and take their input to heart.

8. Clearly define your business. This is not as obvious as it may seem. Write a clear description of what you do. Anyone who picks up the plan—even if they know nothing else about your specific business—should be able to understand what you're in business to accomplish.

9. Develop a marketing plan. Having a written marketing plan is crucial to your business. You need to know how you're going to reach your customers and what you'll say to them when you do.

10. Describe your niche in the market. Clarifying for yourself the specific needs you meet in your market will increase your motivation and encourage you and those who work for you to pursue your vision with passion.

11. Decide how you will finance the business, including your own personal level of investment. Where the money comes from determines who will control your business, so make sure you're comfortable with the sources you bring to the table

12. Determine how you will staff the company. In particular, you need to know who the key players will be and what they need to do for your organization. You should go ahead and write job descriptions for key management positions.

13. Develop a projected cash flow statement. The timing of when you receive and spend money can be just as important as how much money you have. Work this through as best you know. Even if you don't get the timing of every dollar figured precisely on the front end, the process of analyzing it will help prepare for unanticipated variables.

14. Describe the competition. Your business is not entering an empty playing field. Even if you don't think anyone is doing exactly what you're doing (#10 above—your niche), there are others who will seem similar to your potential customers. So you need to know how to distinguish yourself from the perceived competition.

15. Establish pricing. You may need to make adjustments once you begin selling, but you have to have a reasonable starting point.

16. Establish record keeping systems. Since poor record keeping is the number-one reason for business failures, this is critical. You must develop manageable systems to capture the financial and customer data your company needs in order to survive and prosper.

17. Get legal and CPA advice. This is a "special case" of advisors. Professional accountants and attorneys have worked with other businesses enough to understand the pitfalls and opportunities you may not know about.

18. Establish a board for authority and counsel. Sometimes these will be the same group, sometimes two different groups. Your plan should determine which approach you will take.

19. Continue in prayer. You'll need to pray daily for your company, employees, and the decisions you make in order to reliably implement God's vision and to remain solidly on track with Christian operating principles.

THE SPECIAL PLACE OF THE TITHE

God wants the best for you and your business, but He expects something from you in the process. There's no more straightforward statement about what He requires than you'll find in Malachi 3:10–12 (ESV):

> Bring the full tithe into the storehouse, that there may be food in my house. And thereby put me to the test, says the LORD of hosts, if I will not open the windows of heaven for you and pour down for you a blessing until there is no more need. I will rebuke the devourer for you, so that it will not destroy the fruits of your soil, and your vine in the field shall not fail to bear, says the LORD of hosts. Then all nations will call you blessed, for you will be a land of delight, says the LORD of hosts.

People often panic when I bring up the subject of tithing 10 percent of company profits (or more, if that's how God leads you). They fear they won't have enough left to operate effectively. But you and God want the same thing for your business, and Malachi describes it vividly: a blessing so great you won't have enough room to take it in! That should sound good to any businessperson or investor. But note well the prerequisite. You must give God His portion first.

Your willingness to tithe may well be the single most important part of your business plan. I believe you can get by with far less than a perfect plan in many other ways, but not in this. Giving to God the firstfruits is a nonnegotiable if you want to succeed. Get this right. God may even entertain you by sending remarkable messages about what He wants you to do with your company tithe. How do I know?

Charlie, my brother and CFO, once sat with me in my office discussing the issue of tithing on our company profits. We'd been in business for nearly two years and had never resolved exactly how we would handle our giving. Early on, we had no profits, so the issue wasn't especially pressing. During our last few months in Louisville, though, our revenue situation improved dramatically, and with it came the potential for company profits. By the time we settled into our warmer headquarters, Charlie and I knew we were "in the money," and we needed to be of one mind on how we would give back to God.

Charlie had just completed our quarterly financials, and it was clear. We were well in the black, and a tithe on our current profits would amount to about $35,000. When Charlie told me what our bottom line tithe should be, we realized we had another problem. We didn't know where to donate the money.

Five minutes into our discussion about who to give to, Vicki called to say that I had a visitor, a man I had met but didn't know well. Although I wasn't expecting anyone, I could see that Charlie and I would need far more time for our discussion, so I told Vicki to show the gentleman into the office.

The local director of the Fellowship of Christian Athletes joined Charlie and me, and after exchanging pleasantries, he politely noted that he had interrupted us and would get straight to the point of his visit. He explained that the Naples chapter of FCA had planned several new initiatives but needed funding to pursue them. Familiar with the excellent ministry involved, Charlie and I looked at each other, both sure we had a messenger from God sitting with us in my office.

I pointed to the FCA director and said simply, "Charlie, write this man a check for $35,000."

We started tithing that day and never stopped.

SUCCESS, MOTIVATION, AND THE SCRIPTURES

As you implement your plan, obstacles will crop up. Some challenges will come from the natural process that makes doing any business challenging at time. Others, though, will have a special character. You're doing God's work, so the devil himself will throw certain obstacles your way. You are attempting to create something that will cause Satan a great deal of trouble—a Christian business inspired by God, operating to give Him glory in the marketplace—so he won't take that lightly. The solution is to do battle in prayer against him and to adjust your thoughts and attitudes to get the better of every issue you encounter. Here are some mindsets that will keep you going in the tough times:

- THINK DIFFERENTLY AND UNIQUELY. It's better not to think like everyone else. If you're doing God's things God's way, you can assume you'll be on a distinctive path.

- EMBRACE THE RENEWING OF YOUR THOUGHTS. Those who achieve personal greatness constantly pursue a renewal of their minds. Don't just meditate on the right things—do the right things (Philippians 4:9).

- KEEP IN MIND THE CONNECTION BETWEEN YOUR LIFE PURPOSE AND YOUR TALENTS. Those who achieve personal greatness know themselves, and they remain true to their purpose and gifting.

- THINK ABOUT YOUR CAPACITY FOR GREATNESS. Those who achieve personal greatness see themselves as capable of accomplishing big goals. The truth is, we have all been born with the capacity for greatness. Recognize too that your capacity and ability are God-given.

- THINK OF RISK IN TERMS OF SUCCESS. Those who achieve personal greatness take risks with full expectation of success. Risk and great results go hand in hand.

- ACKNOWLEDGE THE PATHWAY BETWEEN YOUR MIND AND YOUR HEART. Those who achieve personal greatness are not afraid to embrace or express their emotions. Let people see your excitement.

- REMEMBER TO THINK BIG. Blaise Pascal said, "Lord, help me to do great things as though they were little, since I do them with your power; and little things as though they were great, since I do them in your name."

Do these things, and you will succeed—in business and beyond. You may not know all that God has in mind for you, but His plans will always leave you astounded by His wisdom, grace, and infinite love for you. He's just waiting for you to take Him up on His offer to make your life a thrill. In his book *If You Want to Walk on Water, You've Got to Get Out of the Boat*, John Ortberg offers a challenge to each of us. "Jesus is not finished yet. He is still looking for people who will dare to trust Him."

I encourage—no, actually I beg you—to be one of those people who will dare to trust Christ fully with your life and business. Think today about what God can do with the rest of your life if you let Him. Consider the impact you could have on your employees, customers, management team, and vendors for the kingdom of God. Imagine: If you had everything you need—money, people, and opportunity—how big would your plans become, and what would they look like?

Whatever you come up with is your vision. It's your calling. It's the opportunity to transform your business and your life into a mission for the God of the Universe. It's the way you will dare to succeed with God.

> Review These Relevant Scriptures:
>
> Psalm 37:4
>
> Proverbs 13:16; 14:8, 15; 15:22; 16:9; 19:20; 22:3; 24:3–4
>
> Galatians 2:20
>
> Philippians 2:13

LIFE—AND DEATH— AFTER HEALTH MANAGEMENT ASSOCIATES

I thought losing Health Management Associates in the public offering was the worst that could happen to me. But God was actually preparing me for an even bigger challenge.

My wife, Cecile, and I reveled in life on Captiva Island, but nearly 900 miles separated our two very young daughters from their grandparents. As a result, we decided less than a year after settling on the island to move back to our hometown.

We bought a charming, early 1900s era farmhouse on several hundred acres roughly 30 miles southwest of downtown Nashville, but during our third month in Tennessee, a hidden threat wrenched us from an idyllic life on the farm. The mustiness of our historic home aggravated Cecile's asthma.

I maintained an office in an out-building on our property, and one Saturday afternoon, a call from Cecile interrupted a leisurely bookkeeping meeting between Charlie and me.

"I need you to go to the drugstore and get my throat spray refilled. I'm really having trouble breathing."

Fortunately, the pharmacy was not far away, but when my brother Charlie and I returned to the house, we found Cecile slumped on the living room sofa, straining for every breath. She gasped out an appeal that I take her to the emergency room—a worrisome request she had never made before.

Charlie and I settled Cecile into the front seat so I could keep an eye on her while driving. Charlie slipped into the back, and I pointed the car down our quarter-mile-long driveway. As we reached the main road, Cecile laid her head on the seat beside me and placed her face in front of the air vent. I heard her suck in a shallow breath of cool air.

A mile down the road, I realized I could no longer hear Cecile breathing, and I laid my right hand softly on her back. My own breathing slowed as I ran my hand down her arm to her wrist. She had no pulse.

I blurted at Charlie in the back seat, "She's not breathing!"

Stopping the car alongside the road, Charlie and I pulled Cecile from the front seat and laid her in the back. I squeezed into the floor space beside my wife to try to resuscitate her while Charlie took the wheel and dialed 911 on his cell phone. We rendezvoused with an ambulance about 10 miles from town, and the paramedics roared off with Cecile toward Nashville's Saint Thomas Hospital. My drive with Charlie and Cecile in the car was the last time I ever saw my wife alive.

In the years following Cecile's death, the disaster of losing Health Management Associates began to make even more sense to me. God knew I would need all the time I would otherwise have spent working on my business to raise two little girls. My daughters were two and five years old when Cecile died, and because I had complete financial freedom after selling Health Management

Associates, I spent most of the next two decades just being daddy. It was the first of two significant reasons I could see that God's plan—even though built on my critical hiring mistake—was best.

After rearing my daughters, I had a second opportunity to "retire." As I contemplated days of relaxation and recreation, I felt God say to me one day, "What do you think you're going to do now?"

"I don't know, really. I suppose I'll play some golf and do a lot of fishing. I'm certainly not going to work anymore."

But God wasn't satisfied with my answer. "Joe," I felt Him say to me, "you're not done. I still have a vision for you."

I was clueless as to what He might mean. Nothing had been brewing in my heart that would motivate me to change my retirement plans. I listened, though, to hear what God had in mind.

The more I prayed, the more I felt God leading me to form an organization that would teach CEOs what I learned about running a company based on scriptural principles. I believed God wanted me to use the experiences I'd been through—both good and bad—and start a fellowship of Christian business leaders.

I realized that I had never actually finished what I attempted to do with Health Management Associates. I had established the Bible as the basis of my business operations, but by making a bad decision I had lost the opportunity to refine my approach. Helping others just may be the way to complete the job. Working through many companies would spread Christian operating principles in ways that implementing them in just one company could never do.

I told the pastor of my church about the concept, and he agreed to call together a few businesspeople from the congregation to get their opinion. A half dozen men showed up at our first meeting. They liked my vision for teaching business principles based on Scripture, and we decided to call ourselves CEO Fellowship.

In the decade that followed, more than 500 men and women participated in our group. Embracing the principles we taught, they moved on to establish biblical principles in their businesses.

As I taught these business leaders—50 to 100 every Friday morning—I grew to realize that men and women running companies were very alone. The have few people in whom they can confide their thoughts and concerns. They need advisors, and they need God for counsel more than any other single input. Yet without being pointed to Him, many never achieve the intimacy of relationship that makes a difference in how they do business. Through Scripture, though, they grasp the vision for reaching employees, customers, and vendors for Christ. The people they touch through these relationships wonder why such company leaders are so different, and the door to share the gospel opens wide.

There are hundreds of thousands of Christian CEOs in the United States today. I believe we could change the world if every one of them were to run their companies based on Christian principles, and it would likely save our economy from ruin in the process.

For the third time now, I've retired again—and I've married the most perfect late-in-life partner anyone has ever found. I met Michelle when she was introduced to me as a real estate broker who could handle the sale of my house. We dated and fell in love and were married. She added two grown daughters to our family for a total of four grown sons and four grown daughters. CEO Fellowship morphed into the Christian Business Leaders Roundtable, and I've finally managed to write the book people have been asking me to write for years.

May God bless your vision!

Joe

KEY SCRIPTURES AND THE PRINCIPLES THEY TEACH

People often ask me about which Scripture passages form the basis of Christian operating principles. While the whole Bible is one big story about God's work in the lives and businesses of people, I've listed below a number of Scripture passages that speak directly to particular issues business people face.

1. Be sure you know Christ personally.

   John 3:1–8; 3:16; 3:36; 1 John 2:3–5

2. Bathe every decision in prayer; listen for God's guidance.

   Matthew 21:22; Romans 8:26–27; Colossians 4:2; 1 John 5:14–15

3. Believe in God's vision for you.

    Proverbs 16:9; 29:18; Jeremiah 1:4–5

4. We are all called to be pastors; share your testimony and vision with others.

    Habakkuk 2:2; Acts 15:6–7; 2 Timothy 1:7–8

5. Know the gifts and talents God has given you.

    1 Timothy 4:14

6. Develop your business and strategic plans.

    Proverbs 14:8

7. Publish your mission statement.

    Acts 20:24

8. Business as ministry to reach others.

    Acts 20:24; 2 Timothy 4:5

9   Servant Leadership

    Matthew 20:26–28; Romans 12:16

10. Tithe

    Malachi 3:10

11. God will show you the best way to go and will watch out for you.

    Psalm 32:8

12. Make sure your personnel policies are supported by Christian principles.

    Proverbs 13:16; Jeremiah 29:11

13. Hire the right (Christian) key people; good reputation is crucial for all involved.

   2 Corinthians 6:14–15

14. Call people into your office for praise.

   Luke 6:36–38

15. Stay honest.

   Proverbs 26:23–24; 2 Corinthians 4:1–2

16. Share your profits.

   1 Corinthians 9:10

17. Keep an eye on debt.

    Proverbs 22:7

18. Don't countersign a note.

    Proverbs 22:26–27

19. Pay your debts.

    Proverbs 3:28

20. Use your spouse as a sounding board.

    Genesis 2:18

21. Delegate!

    Exodus 18:18; Mark 3:13-15; Titus 1:5

22. Handling risk and fear.

    Judges 6:11–14; 1 Samuel 17:45–47; Psalm 46:1–2;
    Proverbs 29:25; Matthew 25:14–30

23. Don't show fear or doubt as a leader.

    Joshua 1:8–9

24. Maintain your perspective on money.

    Matthew 6:24

25. Keep good accounting records and report them.

    Proverbs 27:23–24; 2 Timothy 2:23

26. Use an advisory board; have accountability partners.

    Proverbs 15:22; 19:20; Ecclesiastes 4:13

27. Check facts before making a decision.

    Proverbs 14:15

28. Make the right decisions.

    Proverbs 2:9–13

29. Be realistic when things go wrong; develop plans for correction.

    Proverbs 18:13; 23:23; 27:23–24

30. Don't rush to court.

    Proverbs 25:8–10

31. Cut your losses.

    Luke 13:7; Proverbs 18:13; 28:13; John 15:1–2

CHRISTIAN CEO PLEDGE

Before God and for the benefit of my family and the business to which God has called me, I, _____,
affirm the principles below and pledge to fulfill them in my daily lifestyle.

The Christian Executive Officer . . .

Believes Jesus Christ is the Son of God and has personally accepted His gift of salvation.

Believes the Bible is God's inspired revelation to man and endeavors to live in obedience to its principles and commands.

Is a member in good standing of a local church and supports the pastor and the work of Christ through the church by time, talents, and financial resources.

The Christian Executive Officer strives through the company...

To share the gospel of Jesus Christ with its employees and also its customers, competitors, suppliers, and other business contacts.

To take an active part in the development of the spiritual life and Christian testimony of its employees.

To operate in accordance with the commands and principles of Scripture in dealing with its finances, in handling its personnel, and in administering its policies.

To regularly give a portion of its financial and personnel resources in meeting various Christian responsibilities in accordance with Scripture. This pertains to the needs of its employees as well as others and may be accomplished through direct gifts or through contributions to agencies and ministries.

The Christian Executive Officer exemplifies before family and all others...

There is one God, eternally existing in three persons: the Father, the Son, and the Holy Spirit.

The Bible is God's written and inspired revelation to man and is the primary authority for man's life. Knowledge and wisdom are gained through the habit of daily study.

The deity of Jesus Christ, His virgin birth, sinless life, miracles, death on the Cross to provide redemption, Resurrection, bodily ascension into heaven, present ministry of intercession for us, and His return to earth in power and glory.

The personality and deity of the Holy Spirit, His power to perform the miracle of the new birth in unbelievers and to indwell believers, enabling them to live a godly life.

Man was created in the image of God, and because of sin was alienated from God, that alienation can be removed only by accepting through faith God's gift of salvation, which was made possible by Christ's atoning death and bodily Resurrection.

Jesus Christ is the Head of the Church, and all believers are to assemble together regularly for worship, for edification through Scripture, and for mutual encouragement.

Jesus Christ commanded all believers to proclaim the gospel throughout the world and to disciple men of every nation. The fulfillment of that Great Commission requires that all worldly and personal ambitions be subordinated to a total commitment to Him who loved us and gave Himself for us (Ephesians 5:2).

I affirm this before God and the witness of my signature

this _____ day of _____ , 20 _____
   (Date)   (Month)   (Year)

in _____ , _____ .
                (City)   (State)

_____

_____
              (Name and Title)

OTHER NEW HOPE LEADERSHIP RESOURCES

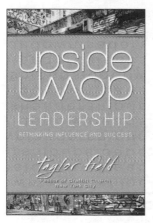

ISBN: 978-1-59669-342-5
N124147
$14.99

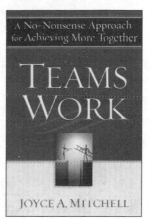

ISBN: 978-1-59669-211-4
N084136
$10.99

ISBN: 978-1-59669-375-3
N134116
16.99

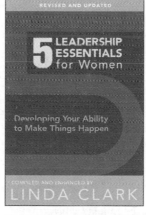

ISBN: 978-1-59669-431-6
N154110
$15.99

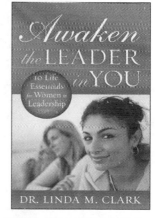

ISBN: 978-1-59669-221-3
N084144
$12.99

NEW HOPE
PUBLISHERS
Gospel-Centered. Missions-Driven.

For more information, including where to purchase, please visit **NewHopePublishers.com**.

New Hope® Publishers is a division of WMU®, an international organization that challenges Christian believers to understand and be radically involved in God's mission. For more information about WMU, go to wmu.com. More information about New Hope books may be found at *NewHopePublishers .com*. New Hope books may be purchased at your local bookstore.

USE THE QR READER ON YOUR SMARTPHONE TO VISIT US ONLINE AT NEWHOPEPUBLISHERS.COM.

If you've been blessed by this book, we would like to hear your story.
The publisher and author welcome your comments and suggestions at:

NEWHOPEREADER@WMU.ORG.